LETTERS TO T. E. LAWRENCE

LETTERS

to

T. E. LAWRENCE

Edited by

A. W. LAWRENCE

LONDON
JONATHAN CAPE 30 BEDFORD SQUARE

FIRST PUBLISHED 1962

© 1962 BY A. W. LAWRENCE

PRINTED IN GREAT BRITAIN IN THE CITY OF OXFORD
AT THE ALDEN PRESS
ON PAPER MADE BY JOHN DICKINSON & CO. LTD
BOUND BY A. W. BAIN & CO. LTD, LONDON

CONTENTS

REPRODUCTIONS

Holograph letters from Winston Churchill, Joseph Conrad, Augustus John, Rudyard Kipling, Siegfried Sassoon and G. B. Shaw are reproduced facing pages 24, 25, 120, 121, 160 and 161

PREFACE

In recent years, my brother has been inadequately portrayed or misportrayed in books and on the stage, and if he is made the subject of a film the limitations of that medium will, at the best, entail an extreme simplification of the character. As a corrective, I am publishing some letters to him (selected from the very large number preserved) in the belief that they will throw light upon the recipient no less than upon the writers. To me, at any rate, his personality is reflected distinctly by the collection as a whole; to readers who did not know him, it may perhaps be more or less obscured. They should, however, be able to visualize the image which each writer had formed of his correspondent. In some cases the image may be seen to have changed as a result of deepening acquaintance; in several instances, too, a series of letters begins with one written before any meeting took place and is continued over many years of close friendship. At the opposite extreme, a few of the writers never met or barely got to know their correspondent, yet their letters contribute to his portrait in one way or another. In the case of Elliott Springs, the American industrialist, this contribution is only indirect; his letter has been included primarily because it reveals that experience of war had affected him in a comparable manner.

I have to acknowledge the gracious permission of Her Majesty The Queen to publish the two letters from Lord Stamfordham. For permission to include other letters I gratefully acknowledge my indebtedness to the Earl of Balfour; Lady Elsa Richmond (for Gertrude Bell); Mr Edmund Blunden; Sir Sydney Cockerell (for Wilfrid Scawen Blunt); Lord Bridges; Lord Tweedsmuir; the Trustees of the Chartwell Trust and Sir Winston Churchill; the Trustees of the Joseph Conrad Estate, and Messrs J. M. Dent & Sons, Ltd; Mr Noël Coward; Admiral Sir Angus Cunninghame Graham and the Executors of R. B. Cunninghame Graham; Mr C. Day Lewis; Miss Dorothy Doughty and Miss Freda Doughty; Mrs C. Elgar Blake and the Sir Edward Elgar Will Trust; H.R.H. Prince Zeid Al Hussein and Dr Raymond Dixon Firth (for King Feisal); Mrs James Elroy Flecker; Mr E. M. Forster; Mr David Garnett; the Trustees of the Harley

Granville-Barker copyrights, and Mr R. G. Medley of Messrs Field, Roscoe & Co.; Mr Robert Graves; Mr W. D. Hogarth; the late Augustus John; Mrs George Bambridge (for Rudyard Kipling); Lord Lloyd and the Dowager Lady Lloyd; Miss Eleanor Manning and Mr William Roscoe of Messrs Shakespear & Parkyn, Administrator of Frederic Manning's estate; Mrs Ezra Pound, and Messrs Harcourt, Brace, also Messrs Faber & Faber, Laurence Pollinger, and Arthur V. Moore; Mr Siegfried Sassoon; the Public Trustee and the Society of Authors (for G. B. Shaw); Mrs Elliott W. Springs; the Executors of the late Sir Oliver Swann; Mrs F. M. Tomlinson; Viscount Trenchard; Lady Pamela Humphrys, Lady Felicity Longmore and Lady Joan Gordon (for Earl Wavell); the Executors of the late H. G. Wells; Mrs B. G. Yeats.

The accurate copying of letters written by so many hands, and not always very legibly, has involved a vast amount of painstaking work. While I cannot guarantee that no errors still remain, I think the chance is negligible. For that, most of the credit is due to Mrs Margaret Anderson, but the copies she made were repeatedly compared with the originals by Mr A. G. Anderson and by several members of the publisher's staff, before my final checking. The only exception is that Mrs Anderson and I are almost exclusively responsible for the copies of certain letters from C. M. Doughty and Mrs Doughty, the originals of which were very kindly given to me at a late stage by Mr W. D. Hogarth, who found them among papers left by his father. Individual problems, either as regards words particularly difficult to read or in the editorial matter, have been solved thanks to the help of Mr A. P. M. Boyle, Lord Bridges, Miss Dorothy Doughty, Mr David Garnett, Mr Daniel George, the Hon. R. A. O. Henniker-Major, Mr G. Wren Howard, Sir Henry Manning, Mr M. H. Mushlin, Mrs Ruth M. Robbins and Miss A. F. Thompson.

February, 1962   A. W. LAWRENCE

LETTERS TO T. E. LAWRENCE

NOTE

The text of letters has been reproduced exactly, apart from the correction of a few obvious slips in spelling or punctuation, and some omissions, which have been marked. The dates, however, are printed in a standardized form, and most addresses have been compressed to a single line of type.

The original letters are ink holographs unless otherwise stated. All the typed letters are signed; minor hand-written additions have been distinguished only when there seemed reason to specify their presence.

Editorial matter has been printed in italic type, and wherever it impinges on the text of letters has been further demarcated by enclosure within square brackets.

References have normally been restricted to the other side of the correspondence so far as it has been published. The main source, *The Letters of T. E. Lawrence* edited by David Garnett (1938), has been cited as 'D.G.' together with the number (not the page) assigned to each letter in that book—the complete edition, not the abridged version published in 1952.

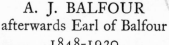

A. J. BALFOUR
afterwards Earl of Balfour
1848-1930
(Then a member of the Cabinet, as Lord President of the Council)

About means of relieving the poverty of C. M. Doughty; see the letters from Doughty
Typed; last clause of first paragraph added in ink. Printed heading

15.iii.22   4, Carlton Gardens, Pall Mall, sw1

<u>Private</u>

My dear Colonel Lawrence,

Your letter about Mr. Doughty puts me in a difficulty. I am, of course, ready to forward an application for a Civil List Pension to the First Lord; though I have abstained — and have always abstained — from pressing particular claims upon my successors in that Office. But, frankly, I do not see what we can do to help a man who refuses — or rather would refuse if he knew anything about it — to have his case openly pleaded! I doubt whether you will do much in connection with a Civil List Pension without a strong backing from persons really qualified to speak about Mr. Doughty's merits, & prepared to do so.

Your scheme of purchasing one of his manuscripts is very ingenious. But is it workable? Mr. Doughty must know perfectly well, if he thinks of the matter at all, that the market value of his manuscript is quite insignificant; and that if he obtains for it a substantial sum, the money must be due to some form of that charity which he would bitterly resent!

Have you tried the Literary Society?

[in ink] Yr sin
Arthur James Balfour

GERTRUDE BELL
1868-1926
(Then an official in the Secretariat of the Civil Commissioner to the British military regime in Iraq)

10.vii.[20]   Baghdad

Beloved boy—

I've been reading with amusement your articles in the papers; what curious organs you choose for self expression![1] However whatever the organs I'm largely in agreement with what you say. I have for some time past been bringing up very forcibly the contention that the argument to the effect that we can't put up an Arab Govt here before signing the peace with Turkey is quite obviously nonsense. I took the example of Syria; Palestine is even better but we hadn't appointed a King of the Jews when I first began the campaign here. We've paid for our failure to make good our promises. We had a terrific Ramadhân[2] with big religio-political meetings in the mosques 3 or 4 times a week, Sunnis & Shi'ahs[3] falling into one another's arms & swearing eternal alliance (against us of course)[4] & finally a serious outbreak in Diwaniyah. In the middle Sir Percy[5] appeared; very wise & sane. We had a heart to heart talk & I drew him up a short memorandum of which I send you a copy, you may show it to Mr. Hogarth but not to anyone else for it was only for Sir Percy's eyes.

I put the matter very moderately but in fact I feel much more exasperated myself than I can say. If you knew what an infernal time I've had here! however I suffer I shall tell you some day.

On the whole the wonder is that there are so many moderate & reasonable people among the inhabitants of this country. I try to count myself among them but I find it difficult to maintain a dispassionate calm when I reflect on the number of blunders we've made.

Now at last we are making a beginning in the right direction but we've not yet got permission from H.M.G. to invite any of the Iraqis in Syria to come back. However Allenby[6] is strongly pressing that Ja'far[7] should come here so perhaps they'll give way.

Now about your treatment of the Ibn Sa'ud question. It's all very well for you to talk as if the protection of the Hejaz against I.S.[8] were an easy matter. It isn't. I repeat what I think I told you in Paris that I.S. is much the stronger of the two. It is only the fact that he has acted in accordance with our wishes which has prevented him from gobbling up the Hejaz any time during the last 12 months. You can't guard the Hejaz by backing Husain[9] & dropping I.S. Possibly you can do it by keeping on the best of terms with I.S. & he certainly, now & always shows himself ready to meet our convenience.

Yours very sincerely

Gertrude Bell

[1] *Most recently, the* Daily Express.

[2] *The month of Ramadhan, throughout which Moslems are bound to abstain from food and drink in daytime, and consequently tend to be irascible, had ended three weeks before.*

[3] *Sunni and Shi'ah, the two main divisions of Islam, are both strong in Iraq, and generally at enmity.*

[4] *The creation of a British Mandate over Iraq had been announced on May 5th and gave stimulus to nationalist propaganda.*

[5] *Sir P. Z. Cox, the Civil Commissioner, had been absent since September 1918, as acting British Minister to Persia.*

[6] *Field-Marshal Lord Allenby was then High Commissioner of Egypt.*

[7] *General Ja'far Pasha al Askari, who had commanded the Arab regulars in the rebellion against Turkey; he returned in time to become Minister of Defence in the first Iraqi Cabinet, four months later.*

[8] *Ibn Sa'ud then ruled only the centre of the Arabian peninsula but was already planning his conquest of the Hejaz.*

[9] *Husain, King of the Hejaz.*

EDMUND BLUNDEN
1896-
(Already author of The Bonadventure (1922) *and volumes of poetry)*

Printed heading

2.viii.23   Stansfield, Clare, Suffolk

Dear Lawrence

Your letter came on. I take notice, & hope I may have the handling of Lowell Thomas's raree-show in Cassell's, lest a friend of his get hold of it — but my Cassell's dealings are obscure now that the editorship is changed. I must myself explain about Cassell's. In the first instance, when the Nation salary was removed from my scarcely gold-burdened shoulders, I gladly accepted H. M. Tomlinson's invitation to write for what he foresaw as a good cheap literary journal. Tomlinson's brother, a man of like passions with us, who prefers Lawrence on the Horse (another Lawrence, I hope one of your clan!) to Noyes on the Golden Hind, did his best to defend quality against the Cassell's money-mad organizers, while H.M.T. went off to Penang. Single-handed, he has been ousted by dealings of which he, though managing editor, was ignorant; & he anxiously retained me, while he was in office, because I represented his original hopes. When articles had been bought from gasbags, over his head, in quantity, he could do nothing. I am dark over the new arrangement; I hope my position won't be sickening to those who have taken me seriously.

Your praising my prose, or rather your saying it had 'a difference', gives me new intention. I shall write some papers, perhaps never to be published, on the Western Front;[1] some on the Suffolk microcosm; some on my motley literary favourites. Not Motley; nor Prescott — probably Felix on the Bat[2] and Darley's Nepenthe,[3] cum multis aliis which if they were to be fully explored the Farringdon Road itself should not contain the books that should be written.

I will maintain that you would have enjoyed my holiday as

14

'purser' on board a tramp. No 'education', nor no Part II of Orders.

Yours sincerely
Edmund Blunden

[1] *He published* Undertones of War *five years later.*
[2] *A cricketing classic.*
[3] *The long poem by George Darley (c.* 1836).

WILFRID SCAWEN BLUNT
1840-1922

In pencil   Printed heading

12.viii.20   Newbuildings Place, Southwater, Sussex

Dear Col. Lawrence,

You need have no hesitation in proposing yourself here any time that you can spare a day or two.[1] I can always put you up and give you a hearty welcome as far as my infirmities of age permit. Any one who can talk to me of Arabia & the desert life finds a free seat at my coffee hearth & you especially who know so much. I was greatly pleased at your letter in the Times[2] and, though I have no confidence in the honour or honesty of our government, I yet do not quite despair of a victory for Asia or the result of the struggle now going on. It is a happy sign that England & France are quarrelling at last[3] — So do not delay about coming & let us have our talk —

Very truly yours
Wilfrid Scawen Blunt

Forgive my writing in pencil. I cannot manage a pen except with difficulty —

15

[1] Cf. *letter from Cunninghame Graham of August 30th*, 1920.
[2] *Reprinted as* D.G. 127.
[3] *The disagreement between the two Powers then occupying the Middle East might give the inhabitants a chance to get rid of both.*

Written when T.E.L. had joined the Middle East Department of the Colonial Office and was about to go to Cairo to attend a Conference, at which his Minister, Winston Churchill, implemented a new policy of self-government for Arab countries

In pencil   *Printed heading*

26.ii.21   Newbuildings Place, Southwater, Sussex

Dear Lawrence,

     A line to congratulate you on having forced your policy on the Foreign (or is it the Colonial) Office & I should be glad to have another talk with you before you leave England again for the East — any how I wish you all possible success in your new appointment.

              Yours ever most truly,
              Wilfrid Scawen Blunt

Upon reading T.E.L.'s letter of resignation from the Colonial Office, published that morning — reprinted as D.G. 157

Printed heading

20.vii.22   Newbuildings Place, Southwater, Sussex

Dear Lawrence,

     I congratulate you on having been true to your word and broken your official bondage. Liberty is the only thing worth a wise man's fighting for in public life.

16

Come and see me again if you can spare a day, or a week end, and help us in the harvest we are making of our Persian roses. They were never before in such splendid blossom as just now.

Yours ever
Wilfrid Scawen Blunt

ROBERT BRIDGES
1844-1930

14.viii.[20]   Chilswell, Boars Hill

Dear Mr Lawrence

I wrote to my friend Tom Barlow about his Greek alphabet, asking him in what stage it was. It seems to me a great pity that two zealots shd be working independently at it.

I send you his reply from which you will gather more than I could tell you. I guess that you will be in sympathy with his 'taste'.

Yours sin
Robert Bridges

I will not answer him until I hear from you. I do not agree with Barlow about Hewitt.

20.viii.[20]   Chilswell

Dear Mr Lawrence

Thank you for returning Tom Barlow's letter. I will tell him what you say — you are plainly working on different lines.

I was glad that my Review of Santayana's book gave you a favourable impression. He is a very good friend of mine, and

B   17

when J. C. Squire and his own Editor requested me to review his book, I could not refuse, tho' it is not at all in my way, & S would think it very audacious in me to criticise his philosophy. The review was quite honest, and I think the quotations shd attract readers: it was my duty to do my best towards getting him the hearing which he so well deserves.

We have engaged a boat at Bablock Hythe for Monday and are hoping to have an afternoon on the upper river. Do you know it too well, or wd the expedition tempt you to join it?

I am afraid we shall not know till Sunday (when Edward[1] will be with us) when we shall start. He is bringing a colleague for the weekend. A wounded soldier — which does not suggest an active oarsman.

It wd be delightful if you came, but unless you came to tea on Sunday afternoon I do not see how we can arrange. Still I write this on the chance.

I have not seen Blundell's 'Waggoner'.

Yours sincerely
R Bridges

My wife has she tells me invited Craster[2] to tea on Sunday next

[1] *His son (afterwards Lord Bridges), an official in the Treasury.*
[2] *Sir Herbert Craster, Bodley's Librarian.*

5.xii.24   Chilswell, nr Oxford

My dear Lawrence

It is so long since we met that I can't tell what you may think of my writing to you at all, or how you will respond to an invitation to pay me a visit. I have heard tidings of you now and again, & understand that you keep a motor-cycle which disregards distances, & it wd be something in the way of a benefaction if you wd look in on us two old folk, for since my daughter went off to Persia my wife and I are quite alone. I was away half the year in America & since I came back have been overworked but am getting clear again, even of the distraction which some good people inscribed for my birthday — really just when I wished to be let alone. Still the public tribute was of official value, & the gift a lovely one.[1] And among the names of the donors were some, & not least yours, that gave me real pleasure. I thank you very sincerely for your part in it and hope that the encouragement which it has given me to write to you is not now making you repent of your friendly action. We do not forget your first visit: pray come and attack these dons again that I may hear about your printing & other projects. You can choose any day, for we have no engagements on hand, except that I must spend a couple of days in London before Xmas. I am sure to be at home: but it wd be better to fix the day beforehand — for see I am already assuming that you will come ... Lunch wd be a good time ... and if there shd be any neighbour of mine whom you wish to see I will ask him to meet you if I have your instructions. I called on Hogarth today & got your address from him

Yours sincerely
Robert Bridges

P.S. Of course if you cd stay the night so much the better

Answered by D.G. 260

[1] *A clavichord presented on his eightieth birthday.*

JOHN BUCHAN
afterwards Lord Tweedsmuir
1875-1940
(Then a newly-elected Member of Parliament)

Typed

13.vii.27   Elsfield Manor, Oxford

338171 A.C. 2 Shaw
  Room 2, E.R.S.
    R.A.F. Depot
      Drigh Road
        Karachi, India

My dear Shaw,

It was delightful to get your letter, but alas! you are thanking me for something I did not do. I would not have dared to write an introduction to a book of yours, and certainly not without your permission. You are the only person I have ever known before whom I feel shy; but I am very glad that the enterprise of the American publisher did not offend you. Your book has been an amazing success, both here and in America, and you must have made a lot of money, which Hogarth tells me you have been ass enough to put on trust for Air Force charities, about which you cannot care a hang. I hope this trust can be broken, for no one is any the worse for having a thousand or two of settled income.

I cannot tell you how deeply interested I am in what you tell me about your family. I am delighted to think that you can claim far-away kin with Sir Walter Raleigh, who has always been an object of my affection ever since I won a prize for an essay on him at Oxford.

I am delighted too, to hear that you are contented in the R.A.F. I rather gathered from Hogarth that you were finding the life in Karachi a little too physically uncomfortable, and that pleased me, for it seemed to make you more like the rest of us. You will be horribly homesick before your term of years is up, but I hope something will occur to pluck you out of the place long before then.

I never wrote to you about 'The Seven Pillars' because I felt that anything I could say about it would only bore you. The copy I received was most gorgeously bound. I never tire of reading it, for, apart from everything else, it is the best work on metaphysics produced in our time. When you do not get inundated with adjectives you are the best living writer of English prose. I gave the other copy you sent me, to Baldwin,[1] and he wrote me a lyrical letter and asked for your address to write you himself.

Politics are a funny business. I have just made my maiden speech. It was quite undeservedly successful. The House is, for the first time for half a century, rather a good club, because there are so many agreeable people in it on the Conservative side. But the quality of the debate seems to me atrocious. Winston is the only first-class debater. The Prime Minister is very tired and has rather lost interest in politics, I fear.

My warmest greetings.

Yours ever,
John Buchan

[1] *The second copy — an imperfect one — had been sent specifically for him to offer it as a gift to Stanley Baldwin, then Prime Minister, in gratitude for having authorized T.E.L.'s re-entry into the R.A.F. in* 1925 (cf. D.G. 291, 367, 548).

In reply to D.G. *565: upon reading* The Mint

Typed

12.iii.35 St. Stephen's House, London, sw1

T. E. Shaw, Esq.
  Clouds Hill
    Moreton, Dorset

My dear Shaw
        I have read your Air Force notes with acute interest and great admiration. It is the kind of document which has never

been produced before about any service. One thing is clear to me, that you are a great natural writer.

The chief interest of the thing is the picture of the impact of this kind of life upon a man of your calibre, who is capable of setting down exactly his impressions and reactions. The subjective side is, I think, its chief value. But on the objective side, merely as a matter of record, it is an amazing picture of the beginning of a new service, for you have had experience which enables you to contrast the new type with the old regular. Your visualising and observing powers are perfectly uncanny. The language, of course, makes much of it unpublishable, and, indeed, unprintable. But that is right and proper enough in a personal journal. If any parts of it are to be used afterwards, you will have to be careful about this particular verbal realism. I feel that most of our people to-day are rather stupid about this subject. If I want to write about a stammering man I do not make all his conversation a stammer, but reserve it for the significant moment!

I have been thinking a great deal about what you told me — that you feel an impulse to write a book of some kind. The easiest form would be a set of pictures and reflections. Your pictures will always be brilliant, and your reflections are the most thought-provoking things I have come across for many a day. But that kind of thing is not a recognised literary form, and one naturally thinks of fiction. Fiction demands a certain kind of shape in the way of a story, for which you may not be very much inclined; but if you condescend to adopt the story form you would write a very great novel. You can write brilliant narrative when you try, as parts of The Seven Pillars showed.

The other literary form I have thought of is biography. If there is any historic figure who really interests you, you would be the perfect biographer, for you can see a long way into the human heart, and you have an amazing power of imaginative construction. I should like best to see you do something of this kind, but who is there among the great figures of the past who interests you?

I have no doubt whatever about the main point; that you have a gift of writing which, in many respects, has no parallel to-day. But the particular literary form you must decide on for yourself, for that is largely a matter of personal inclination, which no friend can advise you about.

I shall send back the manuscript to you to your Dorset address when I get back to Elsfield this week-end. Meantime, a thousand thanks for letting me see it.

Yours ever,
John Buchan

Answered by D.G. 571

WINSTON S. CHURCHILL
afterwards Sir Winston Churchill
1874-
(In 1922, *Secretary of State for the Colonies and for Middle Eastern Affairs)*

In reply to letter of resignation, D.G. 157

Embossed heading

17.vii.22   Colonial Office, Downing Street, sw1

My dear Lawrence,

I very much regret your decision to quit our small group in the Middle East Department of the Colonial Office. Your help in all matters and your guidance in many has been invaluable to me & to your colleagues. I should have been glad if you would have stayed with us longer.

I hope you are not unduly sanguine in your belief that our difficulties are largely surmounted. Still, I feel I can count upon you at any time when a need may arise, & in the meanwhile I am glad to know that you will accept at least the honorary position of Adviser on Arabian Affairs.

With every good wish

Yours sincerely,
Winston S. Churchill

Lt. Colonel T. E. Lawrence

23

16.v.27   Treasury Chambers, Whitehall, sw

My dear 'Lurens'[1]
        I read with rapt attention the long letter you wrote to Eddie about my book.[2] It is a poor thing, mainly a pot-boiler, & deriving a passing vogue from the tremendous events with wh it deals & the curiosity of the British public to know something about them. In fact, when I put down the <u>Seven Pillars</u>, I felt mortified at the contrast between my dictated journalism & yr grand & permanent contribution to English literature. I cannot tell you how thrilled I was to read it. Having gone on a three days' visit to Paris, I never left my apartment except for meals, & lay all day & most of the night cuddling yr bulky tome. The impression it produced was overpowering. I marched with you those endless journeys by camel, with never a cool drink, a hot bath, or a square meal except under revolting conditions. What a tale! The young Napoleon or Clive, if only the stupid 20th century had not made peace. No wonder you brood in haughty anticlimax! I think yr book will live with Gulliver's Travels & Robinson Crusoe. The copy wh you gave me, with its inscription, is in every sense one of my most valuable possessions. I detected one misprint, but to torture you I will not tell you where.
        I am always hoping some day to get a letter from you saying that yr long holiday is finished, & that yr appetite for action has returned. Please do not wait till the Bolshevik Revolution entitles me to summon you to the centre of strife by an order 'from the Imperial Stirrup'!
        All yr many friends always ask about you, & I wish I had more news to tell them.

                                        Yours ever,
                              Winston S. Churchill

July 17. 1922

My dear Lawrence,

I very much regret your decision to quit our small group in the Middle East Department of the Colonial Office. Your help in all matters and your guidance in many has been invaluable to me & to your colleagues I should have been glad if you would have stayed with us longer.

I hope you are not unduly sanguine in your belief that our difficulties are largely surmounted. Still, I feel I can count upon you at any time when a need may arise, & in the meanwhile I am glad to know that you will accept at least the honorary position of Adviser on Arabian Affairs.

With every good wish,
yours sincerely
Winston S. Churchill

Lt Col T. E. Lawrence.

OSWALDS,
BISHOPSBOURNE,
KENT.

TELEGRAMS: CONRAD. BRIDGE.
STATION: BISHOPSBOURNE. S.E.A.C.R.

My dear Mr Lawrence.

I too have been looking for the
crown 8vo edition for you. It is
out of print and I have been
unable to obtain even a second
hand copy. I hope you did not
think

I had forgotten. I was on the
point of writing to you.

Next year I trust there will
be a new edition (ill?) of a decent
size and I shall reserve for you
a copy out of my own lot.

I corrected an absurd misprint on
p 217. I know there are two or three
more but I was unable to find them.

Yours J Conrad.

¹ *An Arabic form of the name Lawrence.*

² *(Sir) Edward Marsh, his Secretary, whom T.E.L. had asked to* remind Winston that he's promised me a copy of his Vol. III, shortly to be published (D.G. 295) — *the third instalment (actually two volumes) of* The World Crisis. *The copy was inscribed* Lurens from W.S.C. 1.3.27.

In reply to letter (cf. D.G. 503) *about his* Marlborough, vol. I, *of which he had sent a copy inscribed* Lurens from W., Oct. 1933

Typed   *Printed heading*

15.xii.33   Chartwell, Westerham, Kent

My dear Lurens,
        Thank you so much for your delightful letter. I am much interested that you derived the impression that Marlborough's ambition was not a hungry one. Apart from the impulse to use his military gift, he was quite content with family life, making a fortune and building a home. In this second volume nothing is more striking than his repeated desire to give up his command and retire. And considering this was expressed in letters to Sarah which he never dreamed would see the light of day — many of which have not seen the light of day for two hundred years — it is hard to believe that it was all a pose.
        I am immensely complimented by what you have written and will treasure your letter.
        Now why not mount your bicycle and come and spend a day or two here in the near future. Drop me a line if you can come, but anyhow come.

Yours sincerely,
Winston S. Churchill

JOSEPH CONRAD
1857-1924

Enclosed with a second-hand copy of The Mirror of the Sea *(f'cap 8vo) inscribed* Signed for T. E. Lawrence with the greatest regard by Joseph Conrad 1922

Printed heading

18.viii.22   Oswalds, Bishopsbourne, Kent

My dear Mr. Lawrence,
  I too have been looking for the crown 8vo. edition for you. It is out of print and I have been unable to obtain even a second hand copy. I hope you did not think I had forgotten. I was on the point of writing to you.

Next year I trust there will be a new edition (illd.) of a decent size and I shall reserve for you a copy out of my own lot.

I corrected an absurd misprint on p. 217.[1] I know there are two or three more but I was unable to find them.

Yours
J. Conrad

[1] *He corrected* musicians, slave-dealers, exiles, and warriors *to read* magicians, slave-dealers, exiles and warriors.

NOËL COWARD
1899-

Upon reading The Mint: *addressed to* T.E.L.'s R.A.F. *number*

Adelphi Hotel, Liverpool   III, Ebury Street, sw1

25.viii.[30]

Dear 338171,
          (May I call you 338?) I am tremendously grateful to you for letting me read your R.A.F. notes. I found them even better than I expected which is honestly saying a good deal. Now I'm faced with the problem of expressing to you my genuine and very deep admiration of your writing without treading on your over tender, hero worship, Lawrence of Arabia corns! Really it has nothing to do with all that. I think you're a very thrilling writer indeed because you make pictures with such superb simplicity and no clichés at all, and I disagree flatly with you when you say you're photographic. Your descriptive powers far exceed flat photography. Cameras are unable to make people live in the mind as your prose succeeds in doing, China, and Taffy and Stiffy and Corporal Abner are grandly written with heart and blood and bones. I found so many things I want to talk to you about which in writing would sound over effusive and pompous so please come to London one Saturday if you possibly can.

My play was a great success in Edinburgh and we're opening here to-night in a theatre the size of Olympia which will be very disconcerting. I am terribly glad you thought it good. I owe you a great deal for the things you said about my writing. Valuable praise is very rare and beyond words stimulating. Please come to London and see some more wheels going round if it interests you.

I am enormously pleased that we've met

Yours
Noël Coward

Answered by D.G. 419

In reply to D.G. 422

Printed heading

10.x.30   111, Ebury Street, sw1

Dear 338,
          I was enormously pleased with your letter & so very much encouraged by what you say about my writing that I shall probably inflict upon you the script of a new play I've written — which will not be produced in England, only published. I'd value your opinion on it very deeply — but please if its a bore to you to read plays say so & I won't send it. If you have a minute in your flying visits to London, do let us meet again. There is a good deal I should like to talk to you about.

We could have supper, lunch, breakfast, dinner or tea quietly in my studio.

So please telegraph me a few days in advance [*if you*] feel like appearing.

                                             Yours
                                        Noël Coward

In reply to D.G. 444

Printed heading

19.vi.31   Goldenhurst Farm, Aldington, Kent

Dear 338.
          It's no use you writing me a letter like that and expecting no answer. It gave me tremendous pleasure and my gratitude must be expressed, particularly as I would rather you liked 'Post Mortem' than most people. This may sound a trifle effusive but actually it's perfectly true.

I know all about my facility for writing adroit swift dialogue and hitting unimportant but popular nails on the head and I thought the time had come to break new ground a little. (Oh Dear, self conscious metaphors are fairly flying from my pen) but anyhow I'm <u>deeply</u> happy that you thought it good.

I would very much like to see you again sometime.

Yours
N.C.

I'm doing a very fancy Production at Drury Lane in September, so if you want to see <u>real</u> wheels going round let me know.

R. B. CUNNINGHAME GRAHAM
1852-1936

29.v.20   39, Chester Square, sw

Dear Colonel Lawrence.

   With this I send a copy of my letter of March 1915, to the Daily News, of which I spoke to you.

I wielded the pen ... you have carried up with the sword.

Can we not finish the job, and get the Emir Feisal (may God give him the Victory), or his Father (for him, peace) made Khalifa?

If you are ever in this city, do let me know & come & have a quiet lunch & a talk over things.

Pray remember me to your mother, &

Believe me
Yours very sincerely
R B Cunninghame Graham

Have you seen Blunt? I hope to do so soon.

Dear Lawrence.

You see I have dropped the 'Colonel'. Please also drop the 'Mr'. I presume though, you still retain the rank, & therefore I direct the letter 'Colonel Lawrence', as I write.

Yes, Caliphates grow & are not made. I wrote my letter from Fray Bentos late at night, & after a heavy day on horseback, & many hours decoding more or less idiotic instructions, from the War Office, & had no time to revise it.

It appeared to me then that it was a put up to bring in the Arabs. I did not know that Allah (for I presume it was he) had you in his eye as a Mahdi.

I read your article in the Sunday Times,[1] & thoroughly agreed with it.

Do come & see me any time you like, in 'this, your house' as we say in Spain. Or better still come & take a quiet lunch at the Hyde Park grill room some day, I do not ask you to a club, as the people would be sure to

[End of page: remainder of letter missing]

[1] *A long analysis of British policy in the Middle East and the resultant troubles, published May 30th, 1920.*

Printed heading

31.viii.20   Ardoch, Cardross, Dumbartonshire

Dear Lawrence

I am very glad you made out your visit to Blunt. He is indeed an interesting personality. Is it not a curious & beautiful old house?

Did you see any of the horses?[1] Perhaps you were too much occupied with 'La Haute Politique' to attend to serious things.

Blunt has been & is a prophet, but a prophet, who like Cassandra, was never believed.

His bitterness of statement has largely contributed to this.

There is no one like him. He & Morris were great friends, & Blunt admired him greatly. There are many things, I could tell you of him, that would help you to understand him.

I enter my emphatic protest against a/ or the/ 'Dunsany God'. For a God you must have a heaven — —, perhaps a hell also. Lord Dunsany has only a drawing-room.

You are right, & wrong (I think) re Blunt & the desert.

He only half loved it. The real lover of it, was Lady Anne. She knew Arabic well. I hope her book, 'The History of the Arab Horse' will be published by her daughter, Mrs. Neville Lytton.

Blunt, as you say, is very Arab; but true Arab, and would have made a splendid doctor of El Azhar[2] (do I spell it rightly?).

Yes, I asked them to ask you to the Wallace affair. It was a good turn out.

I believe your mother is Scotch, & so we claim you.

Excuse this long scrawl.

Yours affec
R B Cunninghame Graham

P.S. When/ or if / you come to Scotland, do not forget, this, your house.

RBCG

---

[1] *Wilfrid Scawen Blunt and his wife, Lady Anne Blunt, bred Arab horses.*
[2] *The Moslem theological 'university' in Cairo.*

4.xii.20   39, Chester Square, sw

Dear Lawrence.

      If you are still friendly with the Emir Feisal, & are in Town, would you introduce me to him?

I have been away up home in Scotland for some time.

Hoping your mother is well.

Yours affec.
R B Cunninghame Graham

22.xii.20   Savile Club, 107, Piccadilly, w

Dear Lawrence
            I owe you many thanks for introducing me to the
Emir Feisal.

He is a charming man & the only Oriental I ever saw, who
looks really well in European clothes.

I enjoyed myself very much.

All good wishes for this rather doubtful time of year.
                                                Yours affec
                              R B Cunninghame Graham

I am sending that book tomorrow.

I hate putting 'T E Lawrence' on the letter when all the world
knows you as 'Colonel': <u>Mektúb</u>[1]

[1] *Arabic for* It is fated.

C. DAY LEWIS
1904-

In reply to D.G. 538

20.xi.[34] Box Cottage, Bafford Lane, Charlton Kings, Glos.

Dear Shaw,
            Thank you for your letter. I am hardened against
letters from unknowns, but not against letters from you. The only
thing that really distresses me about writing poetry is that the
wrong people seem to get hold of it; so I was thoroughly elated
to hear that you read mine: I have — like most poets, I suppose —
a large capacity for ancestor/hero-worship; which may seem to

32

you odd or beside the point in reference to yourself: but we thrive on it.

A Hope for Poetry is a pretty bad book, I think: partly because I set out to write a simple guide-book for the 'plain man' & kept on forgetting this & plunging in too deep & then drawing back without having anything settled. Also, I saw most of the few important points after it was in print, such as yours about the shirt-sleeves & oysters[1] — that seems to me absolutely true; though this getting in one's own laugh first shouldn't necessarily make the result not poetry — Catullus did it fairly often, didn't he?

I suppose my period likes Donne & Vaughan because they find themselves in the same position: the metaphysicals were feeling that the new wealth of knowledge & scientific invention, from which so much had been hoped, didn't do them any good really; so they mocked at it with conceits & deliberate superficialities & had plenty of fun at its expense in a sardonic disappointed sour-grapes way. No doubt fashion had something to do with it too: but a thing can start as a fashion and become everyday wear.

I don't think I understand what you mean when you say 'this book' ... 'was not merely explanation but recantation'. I certainly didn't intend in A Hope for P. to go back on the determination to express political feeling in the Magnetic Mountain: only to define the proper relationship between a poet & his political feeling? I should like to know, though, why 'political' poems are nearly always so bad: the original emotion can't be much less habitual or much more explosive than — say — sexual love.

My book certainly would be invaluable if I could give an 'exposure-meter'[2] with it: but I doubt if there is such a thing & certainly it has never come my way. I do believe, though, that the lifting-capacity of certain themes is not made enough of: the idea that technique, treatment, the 'poetic vision', even, is enough, seems to me wrong: the poet can't see more than is there, even though he may see more than the next man: the Iliad & Moby Dick are certain of longer life than Ulysses or the Recherche du temps perdu because their themes in themselves represented & evoked greater life. I wonder is this impossibly romantic.

33

I'd like to send you a book of poems I have coming out in the spring: is Ozone Hotel a permanent address?

Yrs.
C. Day Lewis

I use a typewriter less & less.[3]

Answered by D.G. *550*

[1] *T.E.L. had written to him:* Poets of today feel often that their real feelings are foolish. So they splash something about shirt-sleeves or oysters quickly into every sentimental sentence, to prevent us laughing at them before they have laughed at themselves (D.G. *538*).

[2] *T.E.L. had written to him:* To make your book invaluable you need to give us an exposure-meter by which we could pick out the one lighted window in the houses they [i.e. poets] build ... Do you believe in a yardstick, or any solvent to divide even the very good from the very bad? (D.G. *538*).

[3] *T.E.L.'s letter had ended:* ... if you want to make us really happy, you will expose yourself to the risk of writing some more poems: and for the ear, not the eye. These cheap typewriters do poets much harm (D.G. *538*).

Sent with A Time to Dance, and other Poems, *inscribed* T. E. Shaw from C. Day Lewis, March 1935

Printed heading

10.iii.[35]   Box Cottage, Bafford Lane,
Charlton Kings, Glos.

Dear Shaw,

I very much hope you'll like this; I think there's some stuff in it better than I've done before.

Yrs.
C. Day Lewis

P.S. I see in your last letter you asked me not to send it: sorry, the damage is done!

CAROLINE DOUGHTY
Mrs Charles M. Doughty
1862-1950

About a pastel drawing of C. M. Doughty by Eric Kennington which had been commissioned by T.E.L. — now in the National Portrait Gallery

4.vii.[21]   Hindhead Chase

Dear Mr. Lawrence,

Mr. Kennington has finished the portrait as far as he can, it remains to be seen whether you like it or not, I'm afraid none of us like it, though it is most extraordinarily clever & Mr. Kennington has been so kind & patient devoting the whole of the morning to try and alter it according to our criticisms, but he is so imbued with the strange strongly marked features of the Arabs that it will be sometime before he can return to European colouring & softness of touch. His pictures have interested us enormously, he has such wonderful power & genius — for Arabs — also the portraits of Storrs & Gnl. Ironside are most remarkable, but your death mask[1] is painful though so like you!! There is so much that is like my husband, eyes & forehead perfect, & the pose of the head; but the colouring is absolutely wrong & I don't like the measles he has developed! I know quite well that its only the paper showing through, but my husband has a particularly fair, clear skin. I'm afraid I have hurt poor Mr. Kennington's feelings fearfully & feel so sorry for him; but I cannot bring myself to say that I like the portrait in spite of the quite extraordinary likeness; let us know what you think of it.

Yours sincerely
Caroline Doughty

[1] *A drawing by Kennington, illustrated in* T. E. Lawrence by his Friends (1937).

28.ii.[22]   18, Southfields Road, Eastbourne

Dear Col. Lawrence
        I spoke to my husband of your very kind proposal to
try & sell the M.S. of his Vols. to the B. Museum; he feels, as I
do, most grateful to you for your very kind thought for him in
these difficult times. He says the A. Deserta final M.S. was
written by an Amanuensis from his dictation, as the Cambridge
Press complained of his difficult writing. The resulting M.S. was
bulky & untidy & it seems to have been destroyed.

He has never had much wish to preserve his M.S. — Adam
Cast Forth seems to have been burned, & The Cliffs & The
Clouds he burned quite lately, as taking up too much room on his
shelves. We hunted everywhere yesterday, but can only find the
M.S. of The Dawn in Britain which has been simply bound in
3 parts (about 1250 pp.).

I am afraid you had a very tiring day on Saty we think it was
so good of you to come all this way to see my husband

                              With kind regards
                                    Yours sincerely
                                    Caroline Doughty

CHARLES M. DOUGHTY
1843-1926

Cf. *D. G. Hogarth*, The Life of Charles M. Doughty (1928)

*In reply to a letter asking his advice before T.E.L.'s first visit
to Syria to study Crusader castles   Embossed heading*

3.ii.[09]   1, South Cliff Avenue, Eastbourne

Dear Sir

I have not been further North in Syria than lat.
34°. In July & August the heat is very severe by day & night,
even at the altitude of Damascus, (over 2000 ft.) It is a land of
squalor, where an European can find little refreshment. Long
daily marches on foot a prudent man who knows the Country
would I think consider out of the question. The population only
know their own wretched life, & look upon any European
wandering in their Country with at best a veiled ill will.

The distances to be traversed are very great. You would have
nothing to draw upon but the slight margin of strength which you
bring with you from Europe. Insufficient food, rest & sleep
would soon begin to tell.

A distinguished general told me at the time of the English
expedition against Arabia that no young soldier under 23 years
old, who went through the Campaign, had not been in hospital.

I should dissuade a friend from such a voyage, which is too
likely to be most wearisome, hazardous to health & even disappointing.

A mule or horse, with its owner should at least in my opinion,
be hired to accompany you.

Some Arabic is of course necessary.

If you should want to ask any further questions I shall be
happy to reply so far as I can do so

Yours sincerely
Charles Doughty

In reply to D.G. 18, *in which* T.E.L. *suggested calling on him about Dec. 15th or 16th. Printed heading*

1.xii.[09]   1, South Cliff Avenue, Eastbourne

My dear Sir
          I am glad to hear from you that you have returned safe & sound & successful from your Summer expedition to Syria. You will have been able to judge from actual experience, how far I was right in advising you of the excessive heat in the plains & the long distances that must be traversed from point to point.
          If you come to Eastbourne on 15th or 16th you will find me pleased to see you, and to give any information in my power: I may say however, that all that I know of the Arabian Peninsula is contained in the two volumes which you have mentioned.
          Perhaps you will let me know by P. Card, on which day you are coming here.

Yours sincerely
Chas. M. Doughty

Printed heading

4.xi.19   18, Southfields Road, Eastbourne

Dear Colonel Lawrence
          Your letter was most welcome this morning. I rejoice that you have returned safe & sound from the late arduous and anxious years of World-wide warfare, in which you have borne politically & militarily so distinguished a part for your Country with the Friendlies of the South Arabians; & to think of your passing again happy days in the blessed peace & quiet days of Oxford life.

We are all well here. My Wife & daughters have served as V.A. nurses in the Red Cross hospitals. As for me, though an Invalid and unable to travel & occasionally very ill, I am nevertheless in good health. During the War, unable to do anything else, I have been busy in my usual manner.

We have left our larger house for this smaller one. It is near the R. Station. We have all had you much in thought, & now look forward to seeing you soon, whenever you can come down.

We have a room for friends & hope you will stay with us as long as you can.

My Wife & Family unite with me in kind remembrances.

Always yours
Charles M. Doughty

In reply to D.G. 117.   *Printed heading*

[? 1.xii.19]   18, Southfields Road, Eastbourne

My dear Colonel Lawrence

I am greatly concerned & grieved, to hear of the unhappy loss of the MS of your warlike adventures in Arabia. I hope very much it was in no way connected with your coming down to Eastbourne. It will be a painful loss of time, to write all over again. It is to be hoped you have your notes & perhaps the full journal, and with your vivid recollection & powers of mind, the original freshness can be retained.

On Wednesday I had an alarming telegram from 'H.M. Government, earnestly requesting attendance' at a farewell luncheon to Feisal Ibn Saud & his fellowship.[1] I took it as a command & determined to reach London, if I could: but had an attack of illness the night before & had to pass the day in bed. Next day it happened the Mission were down here & as I could not go to them, they came on to us for tea; & were all very easy & picturesque & pleasant with magnificent robes & gold-hilted swords. Philby[2] also very friendly; & he spoke very handsomely

& admiringly of you and your adventurous warfare, leading Arabs in Arabia and Syria.

Being up all today I have written to Clay enquiring about the blocks.[3]

In case of a Cairo reprint to be published by Duckworth at 2 g. I can hardly suppose that that would hurt 'the Wanderings'[4] which are in his Crown Library & cost I think no more than 10^s.: but absit that he lose or suffer harm in any way.

very sincerely yours
Charles M. Doughty

[1] *Prince Feisal headed the first diplomatic Mission sent abroad by his father, Ibn Sa'ud, then ruler of Central Arabia only.*

[2] *H. St J. B. Philby was in political charge of the Mission on behalf of the British Government.*

[3] *The Cambridge University Press, of which Clay was the head, succeeded in finding nearly all the blocks from which the illustrations had been printed for his* Travels in Arabia Deserta (1888); *T.E.L. was trying to arrange that the Government Press at Cairo should reprint the book and allow Duckworth to publish it in London.*

[4] Wanderings in Arabia (*Duckworth*, 1908), *an abridgement made by Edward Garnett.*

Printed heading

6.iv.20   18, Southfields Road, Eastbourne

My dear Lawrence
            (I drop your formal war-title as I know you like not titles.) Here is the Ostrich egg which you may remember, at last kindly conveyed by Col. Jacob to your hands. I would have sent it long ere now; but my Wife told me she could not undertake to pack it, as there was no sufficient box in the house. The egg I doubt not was from the neighbourhood of Medain Salih where I have eaten myself of an O. egg omelette; & was the gift years

40

after in Damascus of that Moh^{md} Aly el Mahjul who in my time was Kellajy there during every pilgrimage.

I have several times thought of writing before this, but I knew you must be over-burdened with letters to answer, & might be from time to time again called to Paris.

I am always troubled in thinking of your lost MS. As I understood it had been lost at a R^y Station; I have hoped & hope it had nothing to do with your running down here. I hope you can reconstruct it from your original notes. During the War the Foreign Office kept us much in the dark as to the Arabian affairs & Expeditions & even to any intelligible understanding of the military Work which you conducted then with Feisal beyond Jordan.

What are you doing with your Printing Press work?[1] I am afraid you may find it a tedious undertaking.

If you should be this way, there is a little room in this small house always at your disposal and a warm welcome & that every blessing may attend you is the hearty wish of
Yours very sincerely
Charles M. Doughty

[1] *A project, never realized, to print books on a hand-press* (D.G. 65, 183).

Printed heading

Temporary Address

Rosebarton, Rowledge, Farnham, Surrey.

29.viii.20   18, Southfields Road, Eastbourne

My dear Lawrence

A line to say, I have not written sooner, since there has been nothing material to communicate & moreover I felt you must be anxiously occupied by the distressing events in Syria, as well as in Mesopotamia.[1]

41

In the meanwhile I have at last heard from Duckworth, stating terms he had been able to make with the Medici Press[2] and 'they have, (he says) been a little difficult to deal with'. 'They will pay 150 gs. upon publication & a similar amount when the sales reach 350 copies: the price to be 9 gs. & the Edition limited to 500 copies. We (Duckworths) have to undertake not to publish a reprint of "Wanderings in A." for two years.'

Since I wrote the above, the morning post has brought me a first letter from the Medici Press. 'As the printers will be instructed to take particular care and they are anxious to save time,' they ask me to waive perusal of the proofs.

I think there is nothing to alter. I suppose from this that Duckworth has signed the Agreement, as of this they say nothing. I will write to him for confirmation.

We saw Philby here on Wednesday who had kindly cycled with his little son from Camberley to say Goodbye. He was looking well & seemed pleased with his high appointment in Mesopotamia.[3]

We are existing in a troubled time what with outrageous Politicians running the impoverished middle classes & manufacturers to ruin, consequent general miscontent, the Russian peril, Revolution threatened by the selfish purblindness of disloyal Labour, the defection of the Stars' & Stripes' Land, with Winter well nigh upon us & mad Ireland on our flanks. —

We return homeward on 29th Septr. and hope it may not be long before we see you again our way.

Pray give my kindest remembrances to Hogarth, when you see him.

ever yours
Charles M. Doughty

[1] *The French had taken over Syria, expelling King Feisal: a rebellion was in progress in Mesopotamia.*

[2] *For the republication of* Travels in Arabia Deserta.

[3] *Adviser to Ministry of Interior, Iraq.*

6.xi.20   18, Southfields Road, Eastbourne

My dear Lawrence

      I am very glad to have your letter this morning, though that part is much of a disappointment to us, where you say you are not publishing your Narrative & we hope it means rather, that for some reason it is delayed only.

Now about your kind Introduction;[1] following your wishes I have first noted a few Printers' oversights & then ventured to pencil here & there what little suggestions I might have offered for your consideration, could we have talked it over together.

In one case, that of Ibn Sauds Arabs' visit I thought your few words might be misconstrued, so as to convey an impression that theirs was more than a chance visit to me. (In my attempt I have made too many words of it.)

Of the pencillings, will you ink in anything you may like ('for Press') and kindly let me have it soon, so that I may send it on, with my Preface, to the Medici. The printing is now as far as p. 240 of vol. II.

I have not looked at my Beduin notes for more than 30 years. I know where some of them are. I will look round for the rest, such as exist, against your coming.

When the printing & publishing of the Arabia D. vols. was completed, I found little interest was taken in such work at home. I felt therefore I had done therein what was in my power & as the Arabs say I might wash my hands of it; & could turn now to what I consider my true life work with the Muse, beginning then 'The Dawn in Britain' which was 9 years work followed by 'the Adam cast forth' and the 'Cliffs' & the 'Clouds', (when I felt the Country was in great danger,) other many years work, & lastly 'Mansoul', 4-5 more years. To these, since Arabia, I have given all my thoughts & days, all of long hours, till now.

Till I had looked again, in the last weeks, into the A. Deserta vols. which bring it all back again, I could not have passed a sudden examination if questioned as to outside names for

43

instance, any more than I could at once recollect the names of chief London streets, which I have not thought of or seen for 40 years.

ever yours
Charles M. Doughty

Answered by D.G. 135

[1] *The reprint of* Travels in Arabia Deserta (*Medici Society and Jonathan Cape*, 1921) *contained an introduction by T.E.L.*

In reply to D.G. 144, *which asked him to sign copies and unbound sheets of* Travels in Arabia Deserta *and said that T.E.L. was soon going to Jidda and probably to Taif*

14.vi.21   Hindhead Chase, Grayshott, Hindhead

My dear Lawrence
        The books & papers arrived this afternoon & I have written in them my poor signature as you wish.
        Your letter of a few days back was very welcome, but we are all sorry that you will not be able to come just now.
        Churchills speech I read in this mornings paper. The situation in the East does not seem very comfortable thanks to the past imprudent meddling of not-well-informed Politicians.
        Jidda & the Red Sea climate must be now I fear very trying, when the natural Arabs can hardly endure it themselves.
        And here let me say a word as in duty bounden. Do look out for madmen fanatics, at Jidda, & all the way to Taif. Hussein I fear may be not especially popular amongst his own people.
        I cannot ever forget what befel that great & good Sherîf Hasseyn, who received me so kindly at Taif. He was loved & had lately succeeded a brother who was much loved. Probably he had no enemy. But a raging fanatic is a blind & deaf madman.

I hope you will have everywhere a sufficient body-guard with you.

always yours
Charles M. Doughty

I will post the books in the morning.

About the proposal which T.E.L. had mentioned to Mrs Doughty to relieve his poverty by means of a Civil List Pension and the purchase of the MS. of his poem, The Dawn in Britain, *for presentation to the British Museum* (cf. D.G. 151)

Printed heading

5.iii.22   18, Southfields Road, Eastbourne

My dear Lawrence

My Wife asks me to reply to your most kind letter. I enclose the few words she has been able to write, though hardly able to move or hold a pencil in bed. She is suffering now badly from the after effects of Influenza. I have read over with her your letter, with wonder. Such goodness & kindness as is there shown, is rare indeed.

I have not sought reward for my work but owing to the Great War, the times are difficult. And in this trouble, I may perhaps be allowed to feel I have devoted 50 years of Life to such slender contribution as I could offer to the honour of my Country. And therefore of the kind ideas in your letter, the Civil Service Pension is that which if given, I should feel it an honour to receive. And I think it is that which you would prefer for me.

If the Dawn in Britain MS. were disposed of, I hope it may be to the B. Museum, so as not to come to private hands.

Mr Haslams first-hand experience & advice will be certainly of value, though I know probably all that can be said of Rubber matters. My numerous shares, now of little value, are all in the

United Serdang (Sumatra) Co^y. one of the largest & best managed amongst them all.

Our house-rent, with rates & taxes, comes to slightly over £200. p.a. It is built on the Devonshire Estate and owned by the Builders Family. Our lease has 18 more months to run, & we hope we may let it in the meantime furnished, and go into something cheaper & which we should like better, in the Country.

yours most sincerely
Charles M. Doughty

Printed heading

20.iii.[22]   18, Southfields Road, Eastbourne

My dear Lawrence

Very many thanks for your letter received today & all your goodness which I find there.

Such a large sum to be proposed for the MS. seems very much. Amidst so much kindness, may I say one word here. I should not like my personal Friends to take part in it. I should feel it to be to them disadvantageous, and like to an alms which I could not receive. Mr Balfour, now as he ought to be K.G. is most kind at your instance, to be moving in the matter.[1] Meantime I can only feel, whatever happens, the happier.

The 'Observer' article[2] we have only heard, to our surprise, this afternoon, was in yesterdays paper. I did not expect this, & had sent off my corrected copy, with your corrections added, this morning.

yours most truly
Charles M. Doughty

My Wife after much suffering is now better & improving every day. She thanks you, for kind enquiries, & asks me to send her kind regards.

[1] Cf. *the letter from A. J. Balfour.*
[2] *His review of D. G. Hogarth's* Arabia (1922).

Sent with a receipt for the £400 subscribed for the purchase of his MSS.   Printed heading

31.iii.22   18, Southfields Road, Eastbourne

My dear Lawrence
         It has just occurred to me that I have not written an acknowledgment of the cheque you kindly left here yesterday. I have not myself written a cheque since before the War & had as good as forgotten the look of one & what was to be done. Pray forgive my stupid dulness. (I will pay it in so soon as I can go out.)
— Nor did I, I feel, half express my grateful feeling to my Friend, who though very busy himself, has taken so much trouble & been so extremely kind on my behalf.
    Tomorrow I think you are leaving again for the East, which I hope may not be for very long. May Allah have you throughout in His keeping and bring you safely through & in good health home again.
                         yours most sincerely
                         Charles M. Doughty
    I should like to thank the Contributors to the £400. (but they are unknown to me)
    [*Added opposite the signature*]
    I will set about correcting 'Observer' art. for Cockerell,[1] as you advised.

[1] (*Sir*) *Sydney C. Cockerell, Director of the Fitzwilliam Museum, had arranged for the republication of the review in a limited edition.*

29.x.22   18, Southfields Road, Eastbourne

My dear Lawrence
        I hope this will reach you, as I am not sure of your
private address, indeed until lately, when I read in the newspapers
that you had resigned from the Colonial Office, I thought you
were flown over to Bagdad & were in Mesopotamia.

This is to convey something of the gratitude I feel for your so
much goodness & kindness which I think I can recognise in the
matter of the pension which has been accorded me. This I heard
on Wednesday last from Downing Street, and should have written
at once, but was quite laid up in bed.

It is the full £150 pension as from April last, a help indeed;
though I do not altogether like taking up so much of Taxpayers'
money.

Is there any hope of our seeing you this way before very long?
With all our kindest regards

                              yours very sincerely
                              Charles M. Doughty

14.xii.22   18, Southfields Road, Eastbourne

My dear Lawrence
        Thank you for your kind letter. As for me I have
had a sharp attack of illness, but am now well again. Unluckily it
was just then when Abdullah came this way with Philby,[1] and I
was too ill even to be told of their visit. Philby has a little son at
school here, & the parents come to Eastbourne occasionally to
see him. So he was here again last Sunday and looked in.

Abdullah, he told us, was not much pleased with anything he saw here in England. He could not approve of the endless movement & rush of human life in these parts. He esteemed himself a great personage; & the only thing that quite pleased him, was his seeing the late Wilfred Blunts, (now his daughters,) Arab mares. P. does not like the look of things in the East. He has now, he told me, been able to collect quite a number of flint implements, from the continuation of the seyl-bed at Maan, above which I had found mine.

He said, he had not yet been lucky enough to find you in London.

We are all of us looking forward to the promised after Christmas Visit, and hope you may be able to stay a little with us. Sea air would not be bad after London foggy days & smoke. I wish I knew what you were writing. I hope it may contain something of the difficult & so successful Campain which you led through Belad-el-Arab.[2]

> yours very sincerely
> Charles M. Doughty

[1] *Abdullah, ruler of Transjordan (afterwards King of Jordan);* *H. St J. B. Philby, then Chief British Representative in Transjordan.*
[2] *Arabic for* Land of the Beduin.

In reply to D.G. 216, *upon his eightieth birthday*

Printed heading

22.viii.[23]   Merriecroft, Sissinghurst, Kent

My dear Lawrence
        It was pleasant to find a note from you awaiting me in the post-box on Monday morning, with kind congratulations, on my youthful birthday.

I am sorry you do not tell me anything about yourself. I trust you are very well & whatever you are now in hand with is I feel sure some well doing in your Countrys service.

You do not vouchsafe me an address-heading to your letter. I have tried to reach you twice or more. Especially I have still in hand that presentation copy of 'Mansoul'[1] which I have much wished to send you, as a token of my affectionate esteem for One to whom I owe much, & of continued admiration for your military achievements in a Country I know something of.

I remain in doubt if this addressed to Barton St. may at some time reach you. If you care to have the book which awaits you, let me have a P. Card with an address on it which may find you.

Always yours most sincerely

Charles M. Doughty

[1] Mansoul *or* the Riddle of the World, *revised edition (Jonathan Cape and Medici Society*, 1923); *inscribed* Colonel T. E. Lawrence with Charles M. Doughty's kind regards.

Printed heading

12.ix.23   Merriecroft, Sissinghurst, Kent

My dear Lawrence

I was glad to have your letter of the 7th with the address to which I may securely send you the long intended vol. This Medici Edn. is a good deal revised & augmented there being a year's more work in it. Altogether the book has cost me as many years to write as did the Arabian vols. Wishing you all happiness & with kind regards from us all, I remain

Yours very sincerely

Ch. M. Doughty

Apparently enclosed with the preceding letter

Added in pencil   *Printed heading*

Written last Spring   Merriecroft, Sissinghurst, Kent
C.M.D.

My dear Lawrence

     I am just sending out to best Friends the first three 'Author's Copies' of Mansoul (revised & augmented Medici Ed^{n}.) of which one is of course especially to yourself, to whom I shall always owe so much.

I read lately in a newspaper, that your great book on the Arabian Campaign was to be published at first in a 'serial form' both at home and in the U.S. but was yet likely to be delayed. This will be a great disappointment to many who would be eager readers.

Are not the bare facts of the enterprise set down perhaps in some Government Blue-book? If so, could you lend me the Blue-book for a short time, that I may not longer be left in the dark of events in which I naturally feel so much interest.

Now at last after well more than 40 years given to poetical studies, I feel myself almost 'on leave' and at leisure. We are in our new sojourning place & home in a pleasant part of Kent, where we can enjoy the Country Life & the desired 'Three acres & a cow';[1] & where may we hope to see you.

ever yours
Charles M. Doughty

[*Added in pencil*]

I have just been reading again with grateful joy, in my new found octogenarian leisure, your admirable Introduction to the reprint of the Arabia D. vols.

12.ix.23   C.M.D.

[1] *A slogan (based on J. S. Mill's definition of the ideal small-holding) used in propaganda for land-reform from 1885 onwards, and still given publicity up to about 1910.*

29.ix.23   Merriecroft, Sissinghurst, Kent

My dear Lawrence
        Many thanks for welcome and interesting letter with your friendly criticism. The Mansoul vol. has not any predecessors that I know of, since it is taken solely from Nature, seen through the eyes of Chaucer & Spenser + a lifes (patriotic) study of Mother Tongue. I am content to leave it a legacy, to a future generation.
        We have quite a pleasant little Steading here in Kent. The old name Merriecroft, I have left, as I found it. It means merely wild-cherry-croft; (Merrie = Fr. merise <u>Prunis avium</u>,) & is I suppose local Kentish.
        I am still a Beduin, to whose tent no formal introduction, of friends, is necessary. Should Lord Hartington and Harold Macmillan look in some day, I shall be honoured as well as pleased.[1]

                                        ever yours
                                        Charles M. Doughty

[1] *T.E.L. had written:* I mentioned Lord Hartington to you, didn't I, once in Eastbourne? He has just written to me asking for an introduction to you. I've replied that you have moved, and that he needs no introduction. If he can still come (Kent is not, like Eastbourne, a place where he visits of necessity) you will find him very good. His brother-in-law, Harold Macmillan, would like to come with him (D.G. 221).

In reply to D.G. 245, *which said he should soon receive the draft version of* Seven Pillars *printed in Oxford:* The format of it is repellent, and the small print hurts the eyes

For Col. T. E. Lawrence

5.v.24   Merriecroft, Sissinghurst, Kent

My dear Lawrence
        Your short letter was most welcome and especially for its good news which makes me look impatiently for the Postman who shall bring the much desired Book at last. Whatever it may contain, no one has, can, will or shall read it with more sympathetic eyes than mine, notwithstanding any physical obstacles of 'format, small print' &^c. which as I am not blind I will overcome.
    All these years, as the newspapers gave us almost no information whatever, I have remained in utter painful darkness as to your great Campaign in Arabia.
    I need not repeat here former invitations which you know stand. We are here in Kent & I hope to see you again.
                                        yours very sincerely
                                        Charles M. Doughty

16.v.24   Merriecroft, Sissinghurst, Kent

My dear Lawrence
        I return the valuable vol. you have entrusted to me, just as I received it, (its paper cover was rather used & torn) I have taken much care of it & not allowed it out of my hands. My

eyes have served me well, for in much I am still young & small print notwithstanding I have read it to the end.

It is unlike what I imagined, for the newspapers which I searched at that bitter time of the Great War were a blank or nearly so, as to what was going forward in Arabia.

My very idea of the Campaign was that beginning from Jidda — Mecca & on from Medina touching Kheybar the Warfare, in which you took a great & leading part, was upward passing el-Ally, Medain Sâlih and the Anneyzieh in some nine months, victoriously to Wady Musa.

Now all that fog is dispersed, and I am able to view your vast war-work near at hand, with its almost daily multifarious terrible & difficult haps, experiences, physical and mental strains, & sufferings & dark chances that must needs be taken, in meeting & circumventing enemies, in the anxious Leadership of an Armada of discordant elements, as often naturally hostile among themselves of Arab Tribes; until, after two years, you won through to the triumph of Damascus, after enduring all that human life can endure to the end.

I trust, that the long endurance of so many mischiefs may have left no permanent injury to health.

I am posting the book registered, to the address you gave me today.

yours very sincerely
Charles M. Doughty

SIR EDWARD ELGAR
1857-1934

Printed heading

29.ix.32   Marl Bank, Rainbow Hill, Worcester

Dear A.C. Shaw:
Please forgive me if I have not saluted you correctly:
the address on the envp. was given me by Mrs. G.B.S. so I feel
safe over that.

It was a very great pleasure to see you here, nearly a month
ago, & to know that you were a listener to my music: I have read
about you with something akin to awe & never had the smallest
hope of seeing you here. I am only writing to say what satisfaction
it gives me to know that the Second Symphony has a friend in
you.

Kind regards
Yours sincerely

Answered by D.G. 465   Edward Elgar

In reply to D.G. 506

28.xii.33   Nursing Home, Worcester

Dictated

My dear T. E. Shaw,
First, I must apologise for any error in the way I
have addressed you.

Thank you for your good wishes. I am still in the nursing
home.

Your letter has cheered me very much and your description of

Clouds Hill makes me long to share your cottage even though you appear to sleep outside.

I am glad to hear that the 2nd symphony wears so well with you and your friends, but mark you, the 3rd, if ever I am well enough to finish it will make it look small. (perhaps so, and perhaps not).

Last year I recorded the little serenade for Strings, written nearly fifty years ago, which I love very much — it is as simple and pellucid as spring water. I should like you to have that but it is not yet issued. This might keep the 'pelicans' you speak of quiet until the appearance of the larger work they ask for.[1]

Again thanks and with very kind regards.

I am,
Yours sincerely,
(signed)   Edward Elgar

[1] *T.E.L.'s letter had ended:* Imagine yourself girt about by a mob of young pelicans, asking for III. *Elgar died within two months, after doing little more work on the symphony.*

KING FEISAL I OF IRAQ
1885-1933

Body of letter typed in English; beginning and ending written in Arabic — here translated (in italics)

Embossed gold crown

18.xii.32   Baghdad

My dear Lawrence
     I have received your kind letter of the 26th November last and I cannot but send to you my cordial thanks for the

interest you have had of our affairs despite your being at far distant from us. As a sincere friend of us who has ever been our valuable support, I wish you pleasant long life.

I have rendered your salutations to My brother Ali[1] who desires me to convey to you His Majesty's best thanks for the friendly sentiments which you have displayed towards him, and earnest wishes for your happiness and welfare.

I have decided to visit London next summer upon the invitation of His Majesty King George and hope to see you there.

I close by reiterating my wishes for your everlasting prosperity and happy days.

Your friend Feisal

[1] *Second and last King of the Hejaz. Succeeded his father* 1924, *abdicated* 1925.

JAMES ELROY FLECKER
1884-1915
(Then in an advanced stage of tuberculosis)

Postcard, postmarked 27.vii.14   Hotel Buol, Davos Platz

My dear Lawrence
            I am sorry if you really cant come & see me as — well I wont be macabre. Should like to see you again so much. I am miserable. Many thanks for the jovial account of the Row.[1] You promised me some toys from Carchemish[2] — you horror & never have sent none. Too weary for more

James Elroy Flecker

[1] *A riot at Carchemish, described in* D.G. 72.
[2] *Ancient terracotta figurines.*

E. M. FORSTER
1879-

Upon reading the draft of Seven Pillars *printed at Oxford; references thereto have been changed to equivalents in the final text, where such exist*

[*mid-February* 1924]   From: E. M. Forster

Printed heading   Harnham, Monument Green, Weybridge

Have still about 20 chapters of your book to read, but should like to start putting down a few notes on it. I think it's a great affair, and am much obliged to you for allowing me to read it. I told Sassoon, also Mrs. Hardy, how much I liked it, and won't go on to you, because you probably prefer criticisms, tips. I will try and send some, on the faint chance of their helping you. My own qualifications: have written some novels, also done journalism and historical essays; no experience of active life, no power of managing men, no Oriental languages, but some knowledge of Orientals. Have been a bit in Egypt and India. Now you can discount.

Dividing literature into fluid and granular, you come into the latter class. It's not merely your subject matter that makes me say this. You do present (though you don't see) life as a succession of items which are organically connected but yet have some sort of intervals between them. i.e. you give a series of pictures. I see people on camels, motionless, I look again and they are in a new position which I can connect with its predecessor, but is similarly immobile. There never can have been a Movement with so little motion in it! It all goes on, it's never unreal, practically every sentence and word is alive, but life unprintable — in the spaces between the words — is absent. Trying to think of a big book to clear my ideas (no good thinking of small ones) I hit on War and Peace. It's years since I read it, but there's an incident

58

where Natasha & Nicolai (I think) ride through open country to pay a call on an uncle which gives me a clue. There's the fluid. Not the succession of positions, but the actual slide into the uncle's house, round it, and out again into the air.

Your scenery is perfect. Scenery always waits — comparatively speaking. Rum stumped you rather, perhaps, but nothing else, not Azrak. I noted ch. XLI par. 13, as an example of your power to hold the eye and excite the mind, but any thing else would have done. I suppose you know Geology. How we who don't can expect to convey any thing except slush I don't know. At any minute you can tell us what we are standing on and looking at. This gives a tremendous sense of security in your work.

Animals wait less. The fidgetiness of men — it seems, even of Arabs — is remarkable. How far can the granular method present them? With the big exception of pathos, (which I'll try to touch presently) — I find some thing not quite satisfactory in your presentation of the human race. I'll tell you what to do about it too!! Put in more conversations. Inverted commas are a great help for this sort of writing. I have Auda in view particularly here. He seemed to me your most elaborate character, you had taken great trouble over him, but he was always going — not dead but quiet. All your characters tend to go quiet when the eye is removed, including your own character [presentations are what I am discussing throughout of course] Well to counteract this static tendency, while at the same time keeping your method, you should introduce more conversation. Auda — and you — gained enormously when you ragged his epic style. I was suddenly rolling about among you. And in this connection, you'd do well to have more funny passages. ['There was no more fun.' — I daresay, but that's not my job] Turn King Hussein oftener on to the telephone. Shoot your own camel oftener in her neck. Talks and bits o' fun — not sardonic reflections, they congeal — are awfully useful, they are hostages given by the human mind to the human surface. You've got some and you want a few more. I think of what I can test your presentations by: I have seen Murray for 2 minutes, Feisal for 10, Storrs for an hour, and all years ago. 'Yes, he does them all right' is my valuable verdict, 'but they give out something he hasn't given them'.

59

Well well, this leads me to your style. Discount an under-graduate petulance here. I do not think it is a Cambridge style. And I disagree hotly with the gauntlet thrown down in 1. 2.[1] I'm damned if I ever lift a phrase of yours knowingly though my loyalty to your book is real and will be lasting: have never read a book with such sympathy: am not sympathetic to Tolstoy — — Well. Book being lengthy, you have very rightly several styles, one for R.E.8s, and that sort of thing, another for normal narra-tive, another for reflections, another for crises of emotion or beauty. The criticism I'd offer is that your reflective style is not properly under control. Almost at once, when you describe your thoughts, you become obscure, and the slightly strained sense which you then (not habitually) lend words, does not bring your sentence the richness you intended, imparts not colour but gumminess. Take a very small example. xciii. 15. Awfully good on the whole — real and beautiful, makes one feel that one might have had the experience. But I don't like 'typical'. It holds me up. 'Typical of what?' I am led to say, before realising that the most usual shade of the word has not been employed. Something else v. small — xc. 2.[2] a paragraph practical for the most part, but just at its end introducing a 'thought' and with it obscurity — I think an obscurity of logic (if you are sensitive to manner and if the Arab Staff has our habits (i.e. manners) why should you dread living with them? — — is the sort of muddle induced in my mind). I will go on niggling at small points. It's the only way a critic can possibly be of the least use, as far as your experience goes. I'll analyse a paragraph I think bad — 64. 9.[3]

It starts with a metaphor of the sort I don't much like — a rhetorical allusion to poetry for a historical purpose, which will only be justified, will only pay its way, if it oils the sentence's wheels. This it fails to do. I am pulled up by 'contestants' a little, and a good deal more by a 'cogged charm'. Is the apple cogged, or is a die being thrown for the privilege of picking it up? The second sentence raises no such questions. It runs through on pure poetry and from far far away — from ch. iii to be precise. I like it, but, by throwing me off my guard, it is going to increase my trouble over sentence three. Here Clio is herself again. She opens as a company-promoter, coquets for a word or two with some charm or vision, and then re enters the vegetable kingdom. Of what is this here new growth a client suitor or sucker? Can't decide. Of England, of the Arabs, or of the original apple (control of Arabs)? And — though it's a smaller point — client as adj. is unusual, my mind has had to do that extra work. I think the par. means that the Franco-British understanding practically left the control of an Arab movement to England and that England was well advised to exercise such control. But I've had to read it over several times. It strikes me as an example of the pseudo-reflection, of the process of incrustation going on mechanically, without the writer's full consciousness, and ∴ adding nothing to his effect. If you think this silly criticism — and you'll know at once — you can forget it. If you think there's anything in it, I suggest you go through some other backwater paragraphs (which are necessarily numerous in such a work) and see if you can't make them go more simply. Dont let the reflective apparatus function unless it has something to reflect about.

In chs. XXIII and XCIX-C it has to function. Both — especially XCIX-C — are awfully important as the rare occasions when you attempt to give direct information about your own character. Here, again, I don't always see that which you are willing to reveal, but rather your hand straying towards the black heap of words, and this puzzles and distresses me. [your character is in itself difficult; but not my job that]. How about trying to do these more simply also? I write with diffidence, and on the assumption that simplification might work here — perhaps it would not work. All I can say is that reflection does instantly have an effect on your writing of English: and that the profound problems of these two chs. — problems far beyond my own experience and imagination — have their counterparts in what I have termed the pseudo-reflective process of 64. 9.

Pathos. Entirely succeeds. This deliberate, succession-of-pictures, method is (as Pater showed) triumphant at expressing frustration or the death of what's beautiful. The very stiffness of it helps, out of its dryness the lyric flower pushes. I saw what you could do over some dead Turks early on, and soon after you did something more difficult in describing the disillusion on reaching

Akaba. Best of all — ∵ a philosophic glory was added — was the dumb way-farer by the water-bath at Rum. Now there comes that breathing sliding reality that I do so love and that is always sliding away from me over a precipice.

I must end these notes some how. There is the tedious question as to whether the book's a whole. Of course it is. It would have been even if some one else had written it, because the subject matter imposes unity, and you reinforce that unity although your personal purpose may have been double. An awfully sad book.

I have written very freely to you, but not deeply — i.e. not about the things I thought of while I read you. They would not have been of any conceivable assistance to you — I wish to thank you personally though for shooting Farraj's camel. I hope some time you will publish the book privately in worthy print with proper maps. I hope you won't have a public edition, because that means cutting, and if anything, there ought to be more — as much more about yourself as you would consent to add; e.g. some account of your previous time in the East would help one. You published a fine piece but far far from the finest in a magazine. Why don't you go on doing this and make a bit of money? I would. Extracts wouldn't impair its or your integrity, I think. The Arab feast chapter ought to sell for a lot. Of course you would have to be very careful to retain the book rights, otherwise 'How I took Damascus' would confront you one bright morning on every stall. Excuse this suggestion, and all else I've written. Best wishes. I am copying out a few passages, namely iii. 6-7 for its great beauty and i. 4-5, and xcii. 2 seq. for other reasons also. No indication of source will be added, but if you have any objections let me hear of them, and I wont do it. No answer to this required otherwise. It isn't a letter. — By the way your book helped me to finish a book of my own. Seemed to pull me together. You have only to go on showing it to people to get praised, but it is itself an exposure of that very process and of all that is second rate in public life. You will never show it to any one who will like it more than I do: its subject and incidentals suit me: also my critical sense never stops telling me its fine.

Answered by D.G. 243

¹ *Omitted from the final text:* Probably something should be said of the peculiarities of this draft. For the style of telling is owed a special apology. As a great reader of books, my own language has been made up of choosing from the black heap of words those which much-loved men have stooped to, and charged with rich meaning, and made our living possession. Everywhere there are such borrowed phrases and ideas, not picked out by footnotes and untidy quotation marks, since great lords of thought must be happy to see us tradesmen setting up our booths under their castle-walls and dealing in their struck coinage. At least, I should be happy if anyone found a phrase of mine worth lifting.

² *Rewritten in the final text. In the original form:* He lived and messed for months with the Arab Staff, Syrian and Mesopotamian officers with Eastern minds but with habits moulded after ours. My spirit, more sensitive to manner than to character, dared not mix with theirs for long. Kirkbride for eight months was their silent companion, either not noticing or not complaining.

³ *Omitted from the final version of Chapter LIX. A comparison of the British and French spheres of influence into which a secret treaty had apportioned the Arab countries:* The control of the Arab movement was left lying, like a golden apple, between the contestants, but the charm was cogged. One of the two powers was given all the deserts — the sources of originality; all the holy places — the sources of fervour; all the great rivers — the sources of power; in the Arabic-speaking world. With these assets it might safely invest for the future whose outlines revealed themselves so inevitably a client growth: though the time of fruit had not nearly come.

In reply to D.G. 243.   *Printed heading*

22.ii.24   Harnham, Monument Green, Weybridge

Your letter has just arrived. Yes, it is easier to write to strangers, and that is the objection against meeting: the illusion of social intimacy starts, and spoils the other thing. But I should enjoy seeing you and think there is a practical reason for it, since you are revising the book again, and I might just possibly be of help. My novel is just done, and I shall be loose in March. If you do not come to town, I might wander through Dorset, and you might come over to where I was for a talk. Bring my letter with you, for I had got the thing more focussed than I am likely to again. You might bring a Seven Pillars also, if a motor-bike will sustain them. Then we could go into the thing. I can't cheer you up over the book. No one could. You have got depressed & muddled over it, and are quite incapable of seeing how good it is. The only thing is to get rid of it and I should feel very happy indeed if I could help you towards doing that. The book is a poem all right, howsoever conceived. (I did <u>not</u> divide literature into active & passive, but into fluid & gran<u>ul</u>ar. Your static method does <u>not</u> build up dead stuff). It's an achievement all right. I can't say whether there's any 'hope' in your writing. I should be sorry to say anything at all about your future. For my own sake I should like you to go on writing, because though you may be better with a rifle really, I am not capable of enjoying the results.

I am glad you like my books. I am sending you one which you are unlikely to come across. Let me know what you think about my trailing near you next month.

I see your financial point. You are in rather a hole, because others will certainly try to make money out of you, both in England & America, and when they succeed you will feel cross. Can't you possibly secure yourself against piracy? Could you not secure the U.S.A. copyright by having a limited (& curtailed) edition printed there? But I suppose you have gone into these points, and got good expert advice.

Best wishes & renewed thanks
EMF

7.ii.27   West Hackhurst, Abinger Hammer, Dorking

Dear T.E.

Thank you for your letter which I was of course very pleased to get. Your proposed inscription strikes me as odd, still it was bound to be <u>that</u> if anything, and it does not seem as odd to me as it will to other people, for I am going to paste it into the book myself, and say so in a second inscription.

I have asked Mrs. Shaw to let me have the 'Oxford' edition sometime, to compare, but she has not answered yet. I will ask her again.

My lectures on the novel are a popular success among the Cambridge intelligenzanettes, but they will be over by the time this reaches you, perspiring and greasy among your mates. It is unfortunate that nothing lasts a little longer than it does. Do you ever think of old age? I very seldom — have scares or moods during which I feel that no new thing can be begun, no fresh friend made: there doesn't seem the energy, the futility of one's assertions grow too evident. And then — gathering one's shambling legs together — the effort gets made, the work is achieved, the friend responds, and all forms part of a successful life: to be thrown away when handed in, like an unexamined examination paper. Well done thou good & faithful servant but don't trouble us with your accounts.

Next month — these triumphs consummated — I may go to Gloucestershire via Oxford, and very much want to see some Alpine flowers later in the year Switzerland or Savoy in June perhaps: if you know where to look for flowers you might tell me.

I am now at the Plumed Serpent and entirely agree with you.[1]

Will write again shortly. I have got myself one of the Leicester Square things and am pleased with it.

Yours
EMF

---

[1] *This and two other novels by D. H. Lawrence were reviewed anonymously by T.E.L. in* The Spectator, *August 6th,* 1927; *republished,* Men in Print (1940).

16.xii.27   West Hackhurst, Abinger Hammer, Dorking

Dear T.E.
[*A paragraph omitted*]
I meant to write you a readable letter, but am slack. So is my
forthcoming volume of stories, yet it will be dedicated, I have
decided 'To T.E., in the absence of anything else' The dedication
can be given a wrong meaning, which you will enjoy doing, and
I shall like to think of you doing it. The matter is decided therefore. One of the stories is a feeble timid premonition of the one
which is with you now and which is yours really, and that is what
the dedication really means. If you ever inscribe anything to me,
either good bad or indifferent, I shall be a lot annoyed. (This too
can be given a wrong meaning. Care to have a try?)
[*A paragraph omitted*]

Yours
EMF

About The Mint. *In reply to* D.G. 352

Printed heading

West Hackhurst, Abinger Hammer, Dorking

Addition to letter dated July 5th, 1928

Saturday
Book finished and is good. Read it all today in the garden and
wood. Kept stopping to think about myself, and that the writer,
if he chose, could be sitting in similar comfort.
If I just say 'book's good — masterpiece' you'll be neither
helped nor amused. If I begin talking about your character you'll

be amused but not helped. Yet technically — which is what a writer does want — I haven't much to say. I refuse however to be sidetracked by the subtitles of Notes. Notes may be literature, as in Alexandria: a history and a guide: or are literature, as here. So I shall refer to the book as a book. The first two parts are superbly written — the third part is a little odd: will come to it later. The style (ɪ & ɪɪ) is constricted and yet fresh — exactly what is needed to express the guts of men, and they have never been expressed before: spirited or scientific detachment or licentious sympathy have all 3 had their try, and all failed. You have got the new view point and the words in which it can be put. I am awfully glad. I can't send you minutiae as I did for the Seven Pillars — it wouldn't be to the point, this is a much less elaborate affair (and according to E. Garnett a much greater work).

Now you give good reasons both for the style [epistolary] and for the matter of Part III, so what I am about to say is empty, but what I wish is that you could have taken up your narrative from the moment you left the depot, described your dismissal, touched on the Tanks, described your readmission, and then gone ahead. — Plenty of reasons, dynastic and personal, against this, no doubt: I am only saying what I wish. As it is, the transition is into another medium, into a sort of comforting bath water, where I sat contented and surprised, but not convinced that I was being cleansed. Your habit, that's to say, communicated your happiness to me. Which is difficult to do, we know. But I think more could have been done if you hadn't made that big leap in time and could also have put away from your head and heart the notion that you ought to be fair, and emphasise the pleasanter side of the R.A.F. before laying down your pen. 'For the fairness' sake' (Part III An Explanation) were the words that caused me to prick up my literary ears, and I am trying to keep to literature for the reason that I am unlikely to be useful as any other sort of animal.

Summing up as such, I inform you that The Mint is not as great a work as The Seven Pillars either in colour or form; but it is more new more startling and more heartening than either The S.P. or anything else I've read.

The two most brilliant items are — after all — in Part III: Queen Alexandria, and the chapter that follows her — 'Dance-Night' — which is so charming, so pretty: these are actually the words I must use. All through the book there's charm: lovely the descriptions of the Park, the Hangar, the final wait in the grass, and much of the smut.

There seems to me now no reason why you shouldn't write all sorts of books. I hadn't, before, known whether you could use many kinds of experience, or whether — as far as creation was concerned — you would stop at Arabia. I rather wish you would make yourself examine and describe women: many of them are about, and reluctance can lead us to profitable discoveries.

I hope to see Edward Garnett next week and then will write again, and shall also probably have re-read the book. E.G. wants it published, he will have told you; privately of course, and I don't see why it shouldn't be or why such effect as it might have on the R.A.F. should be anything but good. Naturally you'll have to wait until you'd cleared out and probably until Trenchard had. But there must be no omitting — map of Ireland and all must remain; the only improvement possible is to make the thing longer in the way I've suggested.

It's heartening because it justifies the flesh through describing it; the reader comes away awfully wise. (N.B. — I don't involve you here!! what you give us, not what you are or may be, is my affair.) It's heartening because it shows that cruelty is accidental and abnormal, not basic: I have known this sitting in drawing rooms & gardens, but you have gone to places where I should smash and scream in 30 seconds, and bring back the same news. A world of infinite suffering, but of limited cruelty; that's what one has to face.

Well I'll knock off until next week. Am very grateful.

E.M.F.

Answered by D.G. 364

6.viii.28   West Hackhurst, Abinger Hammer, Dorking

Dear T.E.
            I have read The Mint again and discussed it with
the Garnetts. I am sure, from it, that you are a writer. I was not
sure from the Seven Pillars, because that was about an unusual
and overwhelming experience: I still think it a great, and the
greater, work, yet as literary testimony it has less weight. The
Mint proves to me that you can write creatively about anything
that happens to you. If you did nothing but go to dinner parties
and buy ties, you would still write in such a way that we should
have to read. (I am not, by the way, implying that you were
exactly comfortable in that camp)

The G.s long for the book to be published, and I am supposed
to be adding my entreaties to theirs. Conscious of my own unpublished stuff, I can't get as excited as the G.s just here, though
I would certainly urge you to show the MS. to as many people
as possible, for its bound to give pleasure and help. The charm
of the thing is so amazing, can't think how you wangle this, for I
catch you at nobody's sachet. When you write 'moon' or 'grass'
or even 'chocolate biscuits' the words shine far out of their
sentences or even their chapters. Yes, its charming. And the
helpfulness — it exorcises certain fears and all the more surely for
not seeking a formula. I don't suppose you'll realise the good
you've done or how, by grappling upside down upon the Devil,
you have exposed his back side.

Poor Stiffy! I thought his lecture far more ghastly than shit
carts, commandants, or maggot-soup. It was done so quietly,
genially almost, it was superb, and showed me a new power in
English.

Now, T.E., as to your 'faiths' one of them, the airman's,
doesn't get through to me, though I think it does to D. Garnett,
perhaps that, rather than the changed style, causes me to like the
3rd part, as a whole, less than its predecessors. The other faith, the
bottom dog's, gets through, and I can follow you here imagina-
tively in spite of the difference of our lives.

Now, E.M.F., and his difficulties about happiness. I was very glad to find these here, and may write again. It is very difficult to put happiness across without the dope of music.

Well — waiting for your next — ladies or fairy tales or even some subject of your own selection: I have the feeling after this great success that you can write what you like:

E.M.F.

In this and my other letter I try to leave the Trenchard business[1] out of my calculations. Not knowing his weight, it is vain for me to guess.

Answered by D.G. 365

[1] *Trenchard's probable opposition to immediate publication.*

In reply to D.G. 365   *Printed heading*

12.xi.28   West Hackhurst, Abinger Hammer, Dorking

Dear T.E.

Thank you for your long and very interesting letter, with most of which I agree. E. Garnett makes a fetish of publication. I think people ought to be able to publish what they like (vide probabilities infra), but the world neglects the good stuff given it already, and no one is under any obligation to add to such. I think too that you couldn't betray the men you were working with; though I don't think you would make their successors feel insecure and I do think the book would hinder the recrudescence of cruelty in the fighting-organisations — it is always ready to recur — and might do much good. — How right you are that those chaps, fellows, whatever one calls them, like to be posh, whereas we are amused by them most when they are dirty, off their guard, and natural. Hence a fundamental insincerity in one's intercourse with them.

[*Three paragraphs omitted*]

Well I'll knock off now — unless I hear to the contrary I shall hand back the O.E. of the Seven Pillars to Wilson[1] within two months of the writing of this letter — Good night!

E.M.F.

[1] *A copy of the 'Oxford' draft edition held on semi-permanent loan by J. G. Wilson, manager of Bumpus's bookshop.*

In reply to D.G. 366   *Printed heading*

4.i.29   West Hackhurst, Abinger Hammer, Dorking

Dear T.E.

[A paragraph omitted]

Yes, you told me you were translating the Odyssey, but I keep on forgetting. If the original is in Wardour Street you will not do it very well. Have you read Eddington's Physical Nature of the Universe? That is a book. I understand 1/20 of it, but you, with mathematics and physics, will probably get it all. I would rather have E.'s mind than any I know, for the reason that he both knows certain subjects and understands without despising it the literary mind. He walks his subjects up to me again and again. I doubt the arrival of Gohod in the final chapters. Still he's fairly optional. We cheer for entropy instead.

I was 50 on Jan 1st, and every sort of horror has conspired to remind me of it the last week, but I decline to be reminded of it since Eddington says I needn't be, and carry forward as a savage if solitary youth. Talking of old birds with red noses, whom should I meet yesterday in St James Square but Bernard Shaw. He was extremely pleasant — very nice indeed. Mrs Shaw and I seem to have got over our tiff. This brings me to one of the objects of this letter — the Oxford Seven Pillars still in my shelves. Your instructions aren't very definite are they. Unless you write saying 'I wish you to keep the book until further orders', I shall give it back to Wilson (a) when he asks me for it again (b) on

June 26th. [Why June 26th? Ah. I can have my little secrets too, can I not?]

[*A paragraph omitted*]

Ever your friend
Edward Morgan Forster

Printed heading

16.xii.29   West Hackhurst, Abinger Hammer, Dorking

Not sending Joyce as it's Xmas, and am not sure of the change in your address

Dear T.E.,
Thank you for Joyce, which I return. I expect it is lovely, indeed I like it, though with little understanding. Piccoli, Italian professor at Cambridge, was interesting about some vocal records which Joyce has made, and which are in London, in the custody of a man named C. K. Ogden [*Omission*].

I have been thinking a bit about you and writing lately. I wish you would do Roger Casement — just a personal wish — . Also I think of a remark of mine which you once approved and which has become yours in my mind. It was about love, how over-rated and over-written it is, and how the relation one would like between people is a mixture of friendliness and lust. $F+L = \frac{L}{X}$ is the sort of thing I want you to work out, but of course have put the equation wrong. I think love has an absurd réclame: but this again may be my age. There's so much new to be said about human relationships now that the sac of lust has been dissected and been discovered to be such a small and innocuous reservoir. — — Well you see my point, though by now you are scarcely agreeing with me, perhaps. What I want from you is something about the feelings that occur between people: a novel perhaps. In your so-called (and justly called) faithful recording, you alter names, melt characters together, and fudge incidents. You've only to push it all a bit further, and you're there. I trust that the

Odyssey, to which I feel unreasonably frivolous, nears comple-
tion. I see no reason you shouldn't do a novel. It would go queer
and poetic all right. (Don't bother to reply that what you really
do well is polishing swivels.)

When, after the above, you learn that I, after three weeks
thought and three days' work, have written an article on Jix and
Lawrence's pamphlets,[1] you will sneer slightly. It is all I seem
able to do, and I enjoyed doing it, though it was only to oblige an
editor. I meant to write something more to you now about my
own writing, but don't seem in the mood. Realising that I've
done some good things, I'd like to leave as much as I can behind
me, on the chance, I don't mind whether it sees the light of so
called (and unjustly called) day, of course. — I'll write again
shortly. —

E.M.F.

[1] *While Sir William Joynson-Hicks ('Jix'; afterwards Lord
Brentford) was Home Secretary, the police seized, first, some paintings
by D. H. Lawrence, and then the manuscript of his* Pansies; *the
publisher was afterwards obliged to omit part of its contents.*

Printed heading

18.i.31   West Hackhurst, Abinger Hammer, Dorking

Dear T.E.

What I was trying to say is that you can handle a
theme (write a book), describe an action or state of mind (write a
chapter), and write sentences that are awfully good as sentences,
but which are sometimes too carefully wrought, with the result
that the context, and the paragraph, suffers. 'Then the chapter,
and, through it, the book suffers.' No. Literature isn't so logical.
The dessicatedness blows off by the time we get to the larger
items, and in the smallest (the sentences) it sparkles as individual
crystals; but the intermediate, the paragraphs, occasionally bear
a brunt, and move a little slowly and dryly.

This is based on a comparison of the two versions of The Seven Pillars. I had to admit that the sentences in the revision were more concise and distinguished and showed a superior sense for the functions, and incidentally for the etymology, of the words employed in them. But the relation between the sentences seemed to me a little impaired: the correction, though logical, wasn't always easy.

I know you will not agree with this. You will say (i) that it's impossible to take too much care over one's sentences (ii) that your defects as a prose writer spring from deeper causes, and extend more widely than I suggest. Still I thought I'd try to write it out. Your defect seems to me exactly as above defined — no larger. It would disappear if you would take less trouble of the 'craftsmanship' type. I don't suppose you will, for the particular trouble one takes is bound up in the general emotion one has about one's work: for which reason criticism from another person is never really helpful.

These remarks are awfully academic, and on a trivial point: I wouldn't write them out if they didn't arise from our talk last Monday.

E.M.F.

2.ix.31   St. Remy en Provence

Dear T.E.

I was extremely glad to get your letter. I didn't want to break the silence until I had something to send you but had thought of you frequently, and you should have heard from me in the course of this month.

Your news isn't quite what I call good, of course — there's so much I want you to do and you've hinted you might do — but ever since the Mint I've ceased to worry about your literary fortunes: I used to fear you were the man who had written the Arabia book and wouldn't do anything else, but am convinced now you will turn out anything anytime.

My news isn't what you will call good either. [*Omission*] Of work — well, just a tiny brochure which was to justify my addressing you and which you will duly receive. It is the first of a series, the second number of which will be contributed by Lord Cecil of Chelmsford.

I thought your letter contained an invitation, but was too sanguine, for when I spelt it out, 1935 is the earliest. If you could oblige me by fitting Clouds Hill out a little earlier than that, I wish you would.

[*Two paragraphs omitted*]

Yours ever
E.M.F.

Printed heading

4.v.35   West Hackhurst, Abinger Hammer, Dorking

Dear T.E.
        When would it be possible for you to have me to stop for a few days at Clouds Hill? Would about May the 20th be any good?[1]

Yours ever
EMF

[1] *T.E.L. died from injuries received on May* 13*th.*

DAVID GARNETT
1892-

About Seven Pillars. *T.E.L. had written to Edward Garnett:*
Your son seems to like The S.P. Why not give him your
second copy for a Christmas present? (D.G. 315)

Printed heading

Guy Fawkes Day, 1927   Hilton Hall, near St. Ives,
Huntingdonshire

Dear Colonel Lawrence.
I am writing to you, because I understand from my
father, Edward Garnett, that it is really to you I owe the possession of a copy of The Seven Pillars. Thank you for your thought
of me: the book is worth several hundred pounds & I am a poor
man, though compared with you I suppose I am rich.

But I shall not sell the Seven Pillars, unless I get uncontrollably
into debt. For one thing it is a provision, like a life insurance
policy for my children, two sons, & for another I am never likely
to get another copy if I part with this one, & I want to read the
Seven Pillars frequently. So I shall keep it on the shelf & of
course lend it about as much as I dare. I have already lent it to six
people & waited to get it back before writing this letter.

It is difficult for me to tell you what I think about The Seven
Pillars. But I should like to say first that I think it was a terrible
mistake to publish it in this limited form, and that I think you
ought to publish it in a cheap and accessible edition, or connive at
a piracy by Tauchnitz or someone. Great books exist for everyone
to read: they are not part or property of the author: still less are
they the property of a hundred and ten rich men.

And I cannot see anything in the book to necessitate all this
odious business of giving a great book to rich men who won't
read it, and keeping it from poor men & writers. And then to
publish that shameless parody Revolt in the Desert ... That's
how it strikes me: but it is not my business.

76

As to the book itself: I find it awfully hard to judge it. I have read it about half a dozen times through, & dip into it every few days. It is remarkable as it is the only book I know by a great man of action primarily concerned with motives. It has also a very great measure of unity, of aesthetic plan and aesthetic unity. That of course is partly luck in your subject. I mean the fact you did get to Damascus was of great advantage to you as a writer. The developing tension of the book is the best thing about it — aesthetically or perhaps I mean acceleration.

You know of course that it is full of extraordinarily beautiful & wonderful passages & that they will live for ever ... There is no need for me to tell you that or to pick out beautiful things which move one again & again — beauties which will become too celebrated & trite too I daresay one day.

The fault of the book to my mind, is that you are too expressive: you get every shade of meaning & emotion, but you can't quite do it in one language, in one style, or even in one character. You are so supple, so quick, that your language & style lacks stiffness & uniformity. Buffon buttoned himself into court dress before sitting down to write in order to give his work the majesty of diction and impassive formality which a work on Natural History requires. You did the opposite I fancy & slipped back into silk skirts.

So the fault of the book is the opposite of the fault in Arabia Deserta. Doughty cracks all our joints. Getting into his book is like putting on a suit of armour in the tower — rusty after 350 years.

But this criticism of your writing is only a general impression: I can never point to a passage & say: here the style changes; look: — here is a bad spot.

Anyway, it is the only big book to come out of the war; the only thing to which my generation can point with certainty. And what makes it extremely peculiar is that the book is a freak in literature, a freak by virtue of its subject & the character of its author, & the nature of his achievement.

As a soldier you succeeded, but as a writer you have succeeded still better. I don't think luck played any part in that more enduring, & to me, infinitely more important, success. I think

77

on the other hand you had several bits of bad luck, particularly in your later alterations. The omission of Chapter I[1] (I read it in proofs Morgan Forster was selling for a friend of yours called Palmer I think) was I'm pretty sure a mistake. (I advised E.M.F. about selling it) No, you succeeded in The Seven Pillars because you are a born writer, & a great writer. You are the only living man of my generation (under 45) to whom I could say that sincerely, knowing that I am speaking the truth.

Naturally I want you to write more, & to give up your life to writing. It would be interesting if you did, but probably you value success too much to try.

Well, I must apologise for this letter, & for its tone. But though I haven't met you I can't write as to a complete stranger. The curious thing is that I have missed meeting you several times by a few minutes — at Chaldon[2] once, where my wife saw you, & at 27 Brunswick Sq.[3] I'm trying to write a book now, such a good one, & making such a mess of it.

Yours very sincerely,
David Garnett

[1] *First published in* Oriental Assembly (1939); *reprinted in current editions of* Seven Pillars.

[2] *Chaldon Herring, where, as Mr Garnett tells me, his father was staying and took T.E.L. to visit T. F. Powys.*

[3] *E. M. Forster's flat in London.*

Typed   Printed heading

21.i.28   Hilton Hall, near St. Ives, Huntingdonshire

Dear T.E.S.

Thank you for your letter, which I feel I must answer, indeed I began an answer ten days ago, though you will get tired of having two Garnetts, both no doubt firing off much the same judicious mixture of praise and exhortation at you.

I am very much excited at hearing of 'the Uxbridge effort',[1] and shall not be at rest until I see it. Thank you so much for saying that I may. Its existence is the healthiest news that I've heard: — that and your not liking Drigh Road.[2]

I was afraid that you had found refuge in the R.A.F. permanently, as returned Crusaders used to go into monasteries, sometimes to become saints, sometimes only monks.

I was afraid that you would sink into being a sort of Holy Man, or else merely a regimental Mascot. I should have been bitterly disappointed if that happened, for Holy Men are anathema to me; I hate Fakirs, Russian Yogis at Fontainebleau and all who seek salvation by renouncing sensitiveness to life. Your particular virtue is that you have that sensitiveness; your book is only beautiful because of it. No — it has formal beauty, but without sensitiveness it would have been dry bones like Caesar's Gaul.

However there is no danger of my fears being true: you have written since you enlisted and you will write again, in spite of your weakness of caring so much about results.

— I don't take your remarks about my work badly, for I know your preference for rough edges; though it is an odd one, isn't it, for a man who rewrote his book for five years?

But you have put your finger on my weakness; I am too correct. I am like an unhealthy lie-abed woman who has to put on stays in order to appear in public at all. I am always trying to discard them, I can assure you; — but I begin bulging horribly in all directions. [*Six sentences omitted*] D. H. Lawrence is a most maddening writer boring, ignorant, dull enough to make one scream. and then a terrific artist. He is a sort of caricature of Tolstoy at his worst.

It is natural that you should undervalue 'The Seven Pillars' and doubt its finest qualities. Only dogs can return with complete satisfaction to their vomits: — not artists.

But I can assure you that the book has an astounding balance of parts and structural perfection. That is really much the most remarkable thing about it — more extraordinary than that it should have many astonishingly beautiful, moving pages in it.

It is a big structure absolutely solid; though it has a few

F

mysterious dark corners. Any book in which a man puts himself must have these, for we are all rather dark to ourselves though we may seem transparent to one another.

I am glad you agreed with what I said in contrasting your writing and Doughty's. It is a long time since I have read Arabia Deserta. Indeed I have not read it properly since 1915, so since your letter came I have got a copy and looked at it again. I think my memory of it is right.

I first came to Doughty through the 'Dawn in Britain' which I swallowed whole when I was seventeen.

[*A paragraph omitted*]

I think my view of literature as an art is more theoretical than yours. I lived with painters for some years and imbibed much of their aesthetics.

George Moore seems a very great writer to me and Flaubert almost a God. However I think his letters, his attitude to writing more valuable really than his novels.

Bouvard and Pecuchet, L'Education Sentimentale, and Bovary seem to me very great works of art. My ideas of writing, of form especially, are thus derived largely from the French. Is it wrong to suspect you of an anti-French bias which extends to literature, and even, for all I know, to painting?

I won't solemnly try to refute your remarks about 'living contacts are better than paper transactions', because they represent a mood. I get all I can out of living contacts myself but the emotions I get can't be compared with those I get out of books, being different in kind.

I am so sorry that your eyes are troubling you. I expect you are long-sighted. Do go to an oculist; don't be a fool about it. I want you to be able to read my next book. Besides dictation always shows itself in the style. Don't go blind.

Here we had a week's skating on the fens after Christmas, and many roads impassible with snow. My father and mother were snowed up for a week. Since then there were floods; the Thames coming over the embankments and drowning people in basements. Round here floods are frequent and don't do much harm. But we still have water lying in the house under the stairs. The blackbirds are beginning to sing and England is very nice. Have you ever written a story: I mean fiction, made up out of your head?

Do write.

Yours very sincerely,
David Garnett

P.S. By the way I thought Graves's book[3] was indecent.

I like his poetry and his reviews. I think the subject was a very difficult one for a popular book: — or for any sort of book.

[1] The Mint.
[2] *The R.A.F. camp at Karachi.*
[3] Lawrence and the Arabs (1927).

Printed heading

12.iv.28   Hilton Hall, near St. Ives, Huntingdonshire

Dear T.E.S.

Thank you very much for your letter; it interested me very much, but I haven't answered it because I felt I couldn't go on about French literature of which I know little & of which you gave a wonderful synopsis, and an outline of values with which I am in complete agreement.

I didn't write because I had nothing much to say: I have been in the soup with my own book, having made the mistake of picking a subject too big for me. Unfortunately the things one can't do always seem more attractive: that's the explanation of why scores of pretty talents come to nothing.

My father has had a very bad bout of bronchitis — with a high temperature, but he's up now, though he looks rather bad.

I saw him yesterday & he showed me your letter,[1] and a funny one from Eddy Marsh: — the note of it was like the noise of a spinster hen when an egg has been laid somewhere near. They seem to think there's a bomb in that parcel.

It is the best moment of the whole year here. We heard the

81

nightingale two nights ago & the cuckoo this morning. Plum & cherry are white with blossom; the first apple red is showing; the horsechestnut has grown thick with leaves in two days. All the first hedge plants are springing up juicily: they are knee high before one can turn round. The worst of these spring days is that all the time one wants to put them to some special use; to do something which will stamp them forever in one's memory: there's no way. Instead pure idleness.

I really detest aeroplanes which carry letters & not parcels. As you may imagine I am in a great state about this book of yours. For it will have to be very different, & I don't in the least know your range as a writer: how different subjects move you & call up the right language. You repeat I notice all sorts of meaningless & to you sacred, formulas & protestations, about not being a writer, & this not being a book. You may believe them but they won't save you. Mankind may not make another war in which you might express yourself; but neither it nor you yourself will keep you from ink & paper. You are a writer & however much you cling to spitting on and polishing propellor blades you will write. Meanwhile I can't sleep (this was true last night) for anxiety to read what you have written — The Mint.

Yours ever
David Garnett

[1] *Presumably that written at Karachi on March 15th, which said that the manuscript of* The Mint *was on the way to Edward Garnett and suggested that David Garnett should read it* (D.G. 344).

20.v.[28]   Hilton Hall, St. Ives, Huntingdonshire

Dear T.E.S.

For a fortnight or so I've been living with the Mint, which at this moment is lying in the drawer of my writing-table beside its great black stable companion the Seven Pillars. I want to thank you again & again for letting me read it. It has been a great experience. My father has told you that the Mint is a masterpiece. No praise I can give the book will satisfy him: — how then shall I satisfy you? or appear but as a feeble and almost reluctant echo of him?

There is a real difficulty in being Garnett II or III or IV. (I don't know where you start the dynasty!) Perhaps I should write more easily if I changed my name — & should choose Moore. That might help me to pitch my praises differently from my father's. But of course I agree that it's a masterpiece.

My first impression is that you are a queerer man than I took you to be from The Seven Pillars: (you have probably become queerer) queerer & less intellectual. You don't strike me from the Mint as intellectual at all: I see you as much more a man with the gift of words, a poet, an orator, a preacher, than a man of ideas or thinker. Like the Seven Pillars the book is half record of fact, half spiritual experience: my father did well to compare it with Dostoevsky's House of the Dead. Your experience was far worse than his: convicts do not enlist for prison; they do not pretend willingly to give up being men in order to become a chain-gang.

There is an odd streak in The Mint which crops up now & then — perhaps due partly to its date: what I should call a survival of the war-spirit in you. I mean there is a tendency for you to regard all sort of incidents as illuminating & valuable which are neither ... just because you are so keen. There is a flavour of 1915 (a flavour of Rupert's sonnets!) To me this gives a touch of insanity such as I always feel in reading of — battles — wars — religious revivals & similar aberrations of humanity. I see all such proceedings with the eyes of Candide. I dislike your keenness & the keenness about flying. Even if you were a scientist doing physics it would seem exaggerated. But about a new form of transport! But am I sinning against the Air? I like getting drunk on it, like you, driving fast. I did last night in a Bentley coming out from Cambridge.

The Mint is valuable not because you were in the R.A.F. but because it is finely written, & because of its subject: — Not the R.A.F. but an account of the prolonged torture of the individual & his heroic but incomplete resistance to the torture. He even preserves detachment while it is going on. There are some subjects which are too narrow & too painful to lend themselves to an artist. The tortures of the damned, & the temptations of the saints. But the Mint succeeds where all such fail. Generally, pain is an impossible subject, since our minds have been so trained in the instinct to survive, have been so built up from the origins of life, as to be blind to pain. To forget it instantly when we are not feeling it. An artist like you, who chooses pain for his subject, is enormously handicapped. The Greeks I fancy sometimes succeeded; Shakespeare succeeded in Lear — and you have too. There are moments when one merely wishes to see you clubbed to death, & finally extinguished.

The agony is finely graduated of course — with immense, wonderful, wholly admirable art. The form of the book: the way you have drawn out your string of sausages, is wonderful. Beyond all praise from me.

Perhaps I am exceptional in feeling the horror of institutional life so strongly.

I am the most pleased by life, and all its processes — eating — drinking — sleeping — talking — making love — of anyone in the world. They come naturally to me, easily, I am never constipated. In ordinary life this emotion is never aroused this instinct or emotion of a weasel in a steel trap. When I feel it my intelligence falls away, even my cunning is gone, I am tooth & claw as I was at school or in the doctor's forceps at the moment of my birth. So the shock of the book on me has been very great: reminding me on every page of this emotion & making me live through it vicariously which I have felt strongly in the past but which I had forgotten: the emotion of the weasel in the steel trap, biting the keeper's boots. To go back to the Mint. I don't think it could be improved on, except here & there (for example I don't care about the reflections at church before Stiffy's wonderful lecture: I don't care for the reflections about the Air Force etc in the 3rd part) But being born of notes has somehow made the book, has given it the quality of a distilled essence ... It is in every way a work of art, and could only have been written by a great writer (a careless one — sometimes).

All through it there are very beautiful passages; I should have known at once you were a great writer from the 1st chapter.

Words are your medium, words, not deeds, and not thoughts. Words. The Mint is full of beauty, though you have purposely pruned it too hard for many flowers to show — & only rarely, till the 3rd part is there the splendour & the colour of The Seven Pillars. That book was a triumph — this an agony. Instinctively I pick out to remember in the Mint its least valuable, least characteristic parts: — (because they don't hurt) the first afternoon watching the footballers, the sleepless man rambling under the autumn moon at night & the sentry's coppers: — Alexandra in Marlborough House — shopping in Lincoln (What steep streets! What a disappointing cathedral!) I do so in self-defence — but no self-defence will keep out the maddened tortured — torturing — crippled figure of the Commandant. Marvellous!

[*Five paragraphs omitted*]

Yours ever
David Garnett

Answered by D.G. 360. *Comment in letter to E. M. Forster* (D.G. 364): A most queer letter about The Mint. He said that it was a study in pain, and that it had hurt him; I did not think it very horrible anywhere

25.x.29   Hilton, St. Ives, Hunts.

Dear Shaw,

[*Two paragraphs omitted*]

I think you will smile when I tell you that my wife & I went for a walk the other evening & past the Conington Flying ground. There was a plane up: a young man being taught to land.

I enquired if one could go up & we each had five minutes in the air. The machine was a Blackburn bluebird with seats side by side & dual control. I was a little scared that I should die of fear: it would have been ignominious to be lifted out a corpse. Before we venture on any new experience we are nearer wild animals than at any other time: the same shyness & curiosity. Ray & I must have been rather like deer as we walked around waiting for the plane to come down. The first moment when the last little bump of the earth goes & one goes off into the smooth cream of the air — that made me mad: there is nothing so exciting in the world: the rushing hedge & soaring up: splendid. Afterwards I pointed out our house & we came down round it in a steep spiral & I was leaning out, lying almost on my side looking at the odd Noah's ark. We went round twice — that was enough — & came back. I am now wanting to go up every day, wanting to fly myself, wanting to have a machine of my own, wondering what it feels like to jump in a parachute. Have you ever done that? Is it unpleasant? All my sense was blown out of my head in less than five minutes: indeed in the first five seconds. The pilot seemed more like an angel than a man. I reverence him. He stays at the pub. in the next village & I shall get him to come over one evening.

Well is this a sufficient apology, for my foolish words about flying?

Yours ever

David Garnett

P.S. We both went up again yesterday. It was slightly gusty so there was some of the excitement of sailing a little boat mixed with driving a racing car & going to Heaven. I am badly bitten with flying.

21.xii.32   Hilton, St Ives, Hunts.

Dear T.E.S.

I wanted to read all through the Odyssey before writing to thank you for it. But I have been very busy lately having to review books and had to break off from Telemachus to read Jane Austen's letters to a French doctor. So I will write again when I have finished it. But here I will say that I think it is magnificent: it is so full of the beauty of solid things, — at every moment one knows what they are doing, instead of the blue haze

86

of distance in which the other translators I know wrapped things up.

For the first time the Odyssey is real to me, and I get a feeling of the pace of it. You have got that in prose which nobody gets in verse. The richness is wonderful, and there are very lovely things. The Nausicaa meeting has never been done in any way comparable with this.

Thank you very much indeed for this princely gift.

I suppose there isn't any chance that you will come this way on your motor bicycle at Christmas time?

We haven't anybody staying here: — there is a bed if you can stay & plenty of cold water & apples if you prefer that to sherry & plum pudding.

If it is possible for you to come please send a card or ring up as we may go off on boxing day to watch some gliding which I have never seen. I will write you a proper letter of thanks in a few days time.

Yours ever.
David Garnett

EDWARD GARNETT
1868-1937
(*Then Reader to Jonathan Cape Ltd.*)

In reply to D.G. 167

9.ix.22   19, Pond Place, Chelsea, sw3

I was glad this morning to get your letter. I thought you might have been claimed by Irak, or transferred somewhere or other.

I must have expressed myself badly about 'the heavy father' feeling. It was not called out by passages giving (sentimental) impressions of yourself. It was merely professional delight at your achievement. — plus a sort of personal gratitude for it. (You might feel the same towards H. Melville, say, if you had him in the flesh.)

Yes that's it. The first abridged book if it comes off, must be edited for artistic reasons. But I want you to understand my desire for you & my view of you. Why I want you to write, & why you must write later on is this: I will put it objectively. Supposing you heard a new composer & recognized at once in the fibres of the work that he was doing something nobody had done before, a new approach & a new combination of things in him. I feel somehow that your analysis of life may carry us further: there's a quality in your brain that suggests a new apprehension of things, or rather a very special apprehension of things that will be lost to us if you don't communicate it to us. And you can only do that through writing: by 'The S P' & by things to come.

Well, that's your work, this special apprehension of things. I didn't criticize your going into the R.A.F.C. for I felt you are a law to yourself & you might extract from that just what you were needing. And I can quite see 'your study of man in the ranks of the R.A.F.' I can feel it, for I've had myself glimpses of that sort of world on that level. So anything you store up in your brain, any fresh contact may yield that new apprehension of things of which I speak. But manual work will tire you out too much for you to write. I think you will want more & more 'an empty room' & a 'solitary bed' to express yourself.

The 'S P' is the thing above all you've got to get perfected. Its all there, except the relations of your inner world to it, the expression of which is to harmonize the whole, & make it greater than it is. Don't worry about 'the giving of myself quite away'. We've got to look at it as art, here. The (its) complete truth is art. But the point is also, what are meant by 'complete'. If it's essential truth it's great art. It conquers: it leaves everybody else dumb: it replaces everything. It's it. It cant be shifted. You've gone very far in that direction, but I can help you to go further. I can help you, I think, because as to effects I really see what a thing is: & I can tell you where you need to be more of an artist. And in this

88

sense too the expression of the essential truth is really the point, ie the just expression.* At any rate I can tell you that you're quite needlessly alarmed about 'sentimental' passages. You haven't really risen, there just to the imperative occasion. You're flat & disappointing there as art. When I get the proofs again I can show you what I mean exactly.

Well, you've got to work at the 'S P', slowly & calmly. But I don't see why you shouldn't think seriously of that 'magazine' idea of mine. It might fill the place in literature that is now, vacant. As to 'training' that's all fudge. Its merely a matter of task & insight. And you've got these to a degree, higher, I think, than I have. I've never been 'educated'/I've never done anything but things impromptu. I've never followed anything up. I don't know languages, etc etc./

By a coincidence, a man came yesterday to see my son David, & said he wanted to go in for publishing — & that he had got money. He seemed to be a genuine sort of chap, with vague ideas, & money to spend./And I've just stepped out & phoned David to keep in touch with him, & let me see him next week./He might, possibly, be the right man to back 'Belles Lettres'. At any rate I'll see him. And you turn the matter over. To edit such a magazine, would be worth doing. Think it over, there's no hurry to decide anything.

Things shape themselves.

In haste
(catching a train)
EG.

* And here the half often is greater than the whole.

About an attempted abridgement (never published) of Seven Pillars; *a reference has been changed to apply to the final text*

16.x.22   19, Pond Place, Chelsea, sw3

We said a good deal in the course of that debate yesterday, but I'm not sure if I made these points.

1. The text of Chapters xcix-cv (approximately) ie. the first half of the final section, would certainly gain by elimination of detail if possible. I simply didn't see what to knock out, but it needs more harmonizing if possible.

2. You rather frightened me by your threat to impair the Auda battlepiece. When your camel fell & you lay still chanting those abominable Kipling verses. The picture is so fresh & full of sap. Don't mind a little playfulness here & there. Don't take the curl out of the hair!

3. The picture of your bodyguard is very valuable, & one of the best written passages. The MS rather suffers from you always being like a bird in two places at once; here we get a withdrawn interior & can rest a little, & see your relation to your men.

4. Some geological detail can certainly go out, here & there, but I was afraid of weakening the atmospheric feeling.

5. The picture of Rum is extraordinarily real but it is quite true what I said, viz. that each time one rereads it is diminished in power: & that simply shews that what is most indestructible is poetry, ie. the fusion of the characteristic elements in the creative imagination. So, in the subsequent references to Rum we need some poetic fresh detail to reawaken the former impression: ie — if you had seen a bird winging his way against a cliff; or heard the scream of some animal; or were oppressed by the stillness at night, or gave us a feeling of the night wind in the cave — etc etc, the picture would be living again.——

I am keeping the cancelled portions till you come again, — (in case of you needing some passage) when we will have an auto-da-fé together.

In reply to D.G. 180; *upon receipt of the manuscript of the*
abridgement

[22.xi.22]

I felt excited when I got your letter & the MS, &
got down immediately & went through your revision. I felt
sulky, very, when I saw what you've done to the camel charge,
& poor Farraj. I perceived that your temperament had neatly
revenged itself on mine. Then, obeying my instinct, I went out
& bought half a pound of steak — price sevenpence* — &
grilled it, & ate it solemnly, & read the Kid Lewis fight.

Your Preface is good, but there are two or three phrases such
as 'I was nearly penniless' — which I think need reconsideration.
It opens up such vistas of curiosity! 'Why is Colonel Lawrence
penniless?' 'Why haven't they done this or that.' 'Why hasn't he
— ' etc etc. And you cant go into these inner histories However
apart from a few words, the Preface is good & is a valuable
historical document. It has all your queer flavour, as of some sun-
dried fruit, with the lusciousness three quarters dried out of it,
but very sustaining and also provocative.

I'm going to read the whole thing through before I see you —
so as to get a definite, clear impression of the 'abridgment'.

At present I feel sulky at your suppression of the best personal
passages. 'I gave you up Deraa' I say, reproachfully, like a sob-
bing woman! & now you take Farraj's death from me!

I'm not sure that you can delete Farraj. You don't seem to see
that you are only thinking of yourself & preserving intact &
secret these moments. What a world it would be if all the great
writers had suddenly shied off 'wearing their hearts upon their
sleeves'. However, I wont abuse you. 'Master Edward has been
very good', as nurses say to their charges, even while 'Master
Edward' is scowling.

/By the way talking of women, when you can, go to 30
Gerrard Street, Wardour Street (my son's bookshop) & have a
look at Miss Frances Marshall who is serving in the shop./Her

* The steak was tough; so I feel severe.

sister, illustrated 'Lady into Fox'. —/You wont see her with my eyes; but if you have read the old Celtic fairy stories, you will recognize whence those tellers took their portraits of the great Chieftain's daughter./

Yes, I shall read the abridgment right through. It's a wonderful book anyway. I <u>know</u> that; & I daresay I shall walk up & down the room, & say — as I've said before — 'well, imp of the world! You're a creator! You have <u>done</u> it!'

EG.

I take it that you will write, or have written, as to whether you are coming this Saturday or next

Answered by D.G. 181

In reply to D.G. 180 *and* 181

23.xi.22

        I'm re-reading the abridgment & will let you know what I think of it next week. I'll renumber the pages, & chapters, & suggest the divisions into Books. When its in proof you can add the chapter headings, etc. You're an expert in all these matters.

You've revised the camel charge, 'for reasons of self respect'. Be it so! Keep your self respect & rob English literature of a passage beautifully spontaneous, <u>Colonel</u> Lawrence!

I'm not sure whether you <u>can</u> sacrifice Farraj's death. The end of the chapter is too <u>beautiful</u> — & if it hangs in the air let it hang in the air. But I'll reserve my judgment awhile.

The Preface I think, should stand as it is with the correction of the few lines I indicate. I return it you, with the title I like best. Which I think is <u>the</u> title.

I suspect your 'taste' is better than mine but more exclusive. It seems to waver a bit according to your self-repressive mood.

92

How do you like 'Marie Grubbe'.[1] I should have thought that you who are so subtle in action & perception, would have felt very near to Po-Chü-i's subtlety. I can understand that Turgenev is too feminine, too gracious to please the Scotch-Scandinavian-Dutch (is it?) amalgam in you. But perhaps there are other reasons.

I think now the abridgment is done it should be put in the agent's hands without delay.

There was one thing I wanted to ask. Shall I tell Cape about the abridgment & that it is earmarked for another publisher? The fact that I am his 'reader' etc. makes it necessary for me to be clear & definite with him./You can of course, say that you may have something later for him — if you should ever do 'Uxbridge'./[2] Or we can say nothing at all, as, like all publishers he lives on great expectations of the most nebulous order.

EG.

If you know of any sculptors <u>better</u> than Lady Scott please send their names.

Rothenstein's drawings of Hudson are disgracefully bad. R is a master at persuading 'the great' to sit to him, & the results are — to my mind — sufficiently lamentable.

Answered by D.G. 182

[1] *He had given T.E.L. a translation of this Danish classic by J. P. Jacobsen.*
[2] The Mint.

In reply to D.G. 319

18.vii.27   19, Pond Place, Chelsea, sw3

Yes, you immensely strengthened & perfected 'The Seven Pillars' by your continuous work on it. The final form is a very different thing from the double column 'Oxford' version.

There is no doubt at all that 'The S Pillars' now is a 'masterpiece': not in attaining the particular heights you aimed at at first — but a masterpiece in itself, on its own basis — a masterpiece that can never be ignored or supplanted — a masterpiece that will live in literature on its own basis, quite secure.

You have got it into form; into as good a shape as was possible, considering what you had to do, & the frightful mass of details.

I have criticized you severely in the past for your self consciousness, for your hiding of your own emotions, for your subtle evasions & omissions, — & for the elaborate tricks you play & for the 'Peccavi' thrown at us in the abrupt section 'Myself'.

I take this back in recognizing that you are built that way, & that the whole character of the book reflects & is governed by the laws of your own character. One cant quarrel with the individuality that has made 'the S P' what it is — a masterpiece of narrative. Your instinct of keeping yourself & your emotions, so much down & under is justified by the result, & even the glaring beam you suddenly throw on yourself in 'Myself', fits into its place, now, much better than I thought was possible. 'The Seven Pillars' is extraordinarily individual. It holds one firmly from first to last: it is a very big yet exceedingly complex picture, both broad in the mass, & minute in the details — a just, sympathetic & impartial chronicle & extraordinarily truthful. In its own way it is a real work of art, as much of a work of art as was possible in such an historical-chronicle, following your plan of keeping your emotions so much out of sight. I say this despite the fact that all your best pages & passages, are, as a matter of fact, subtly emotional, in your restrained fashion, & that in the dozen or score finest of all, you do suddenly disclose yourself, — but a bigger man than you would have been much more explicit & much more careless about giving himself away. And these sudden breaks & strange free disclosures would have lifted us out of ourselves, & produced a richer, more variegated effect — something incalculable. The version you have preferred is so to say the version of the official you which might have been supplemented by the revelations of the unofficial you, thereby attaining a richer range of colouring. But I am not complaining of this. And I refer to it to say that you have another book in you, at

94

least as good as 'The S P.' & one that should be much easier to write, one that should also be a masterpiece. It should be a book from the personal side, dictated by the unofficial you — a book of episodes, like beads on a string. Say episodes from your life as an archaeologist, of your pre-war life in Syria, your fruitless journey to Syria during the war — etc. You should write it without thinking of yourself or of the public — only critically anxious to set down what you thought & felt in each particular episode. You also could put into it a variety of things you have not had time to speak of in 'The S Pillars'. You are a born writer, fearfully handicapped by fixed ideas & all sorts of complexes, which the great achievement of 'The S Pillars' should have dissipated. Of course it may be the most prudent course for you not to 'tempt fate with another book' — but I suggest that you write the 'Episodes' for your own pleasure as a writer, after you have let me see the 'Notes on Uxbridge' — which is overdue from you to me, if I may make this mild remark.

You see I have come mainly round to Miss Heath's view of 'The S Pillars' — which I transmitted to you half a year or so ago. And should I ever write a few pages on the S P. I should take that line. That you have cut off the public from 'The S P' is bad enough. For the book is now a valuable curiosity for the Cabinets of rich men Collectors who never let their books be read for fear of spoiling their 'condition'. You didn't wish the man in the street to read your sacred emotions, & you have succeeded absolutely.

You may think I am obsessed on the point of your writing again. But I remember what you said about your ambition to write something artistically great. Dostoevsky emptied himself out in 'The Karamazov Brothers' — & if you got into the habit of emptying yourself out either in 'Episodes' or something of that kind, we should have a book of the highest originality. Not one writer in a thousand writes frankly. Those Poems of Thomas are great because he dared to write (at last, at last) frankly of his own emotions, & he knew how to do it.

Get in this habit of writing frankly & begin at once & you needn't then fear 'tempting Fate'.

I repeat that in 'S Pillars' you have written a masterpiece, though for two reasons it isn't on the plane you originally aimed at.

EG.

P.S. I dont care of course under what form or what literary disguise you express your spirit & heart freely, so long as you do express it. I grant that you <u>have</u> expressed it in 'The Seven Pillars': but there is a deeper <u>self</u> in you yet unexpressed, & to be expressed artistically. Rabelais, Sterne, Walt Whitman, Herman Melville, Dostoevsky, Turgenev, Dante, & all the great spirits from W.S. downwards, dont hesitate about expressing themselves frankly. Your 'six years' has produced a masterpiece — so don't make bones about expressing yourself in future.

In reply to D.G. 344 *and* 345. *Upon reading* The Mint

Printed heading

22.iv.28   19, Pond Place, Chelsea, sw3

You received, I hope, my week-end Telegram,[1] despatched yesterday to Drigh Road?

Well, you've gone & done it this time! & knocked all your feeble pretences of not being a writer, etc etc. into final smithereens. I received the precious MS. on the 18th & read it, very carefully, in the next two days & the deeper I got the more delighted I was. It is a most <u>perfect</u> piece of writing. I call it a <u>classic</u> for there's not a word too much. It's elastic, sinewy, terse: & spirit & matter are the inside-out of its technique, perfectly harmonious throughout — inseparable as in all first rate stuff. Its very original in its effect, for having given us the essential in its living body, it smites one much harder than if you had made 'a book' of it, or told us more. That terse, sinewy, yet elastic form, all lean & athletic, is just what is right: the descriptions of the men, China, Sailor, Corp. Abner, Taffy, Stiffy, the Commandant, etc. are wonderfully drawn, mere thumbnail sketches, with the lines bitten in with a marked precision. Then, the atmosphere that grows more hard & bitter & north-easterly as the men get branded, or 'minted' in the struggle. There's nothing like it in the least in English: there may be in French? The style has the just precision of Maupassant at his best; but has of course, quite a different quality. And the narrative goes on justifying itself in its actuality — in its tensity of fact, just as 'The House of the Dead' does, so that one forgets it is a book. These chapters, xv Church, xix Shitcart, xx Air commanding officer, xxvi China: Trouble, xxx Discipline, xxxv Intemperate, xlv Offensive, xlix In the Guard Room, lviii The Hangar, lx Funeral, lxiii Police Duty, lxi The Dance, lxvii The Pond; lxviii A Thursday Night lxix, Interlude. These chapters I single out, not because there are not others equal to them, but because their art is faultless in feeling & in expression. I abused you for not recording your own sensations & emotions in 'The Seven Pillars' — & here you have marvellously fused the whole objective picture with your breath, your sensations & your self. What strikes me specially is the justesse of it all. No tricks, & no self-consciousness here. Just your own sensations & your judgement, impartial, as any one finite man's can be. The book has a perfect spiritual balance. For a book it is. One has no feeling of 'notes' at all. The 'lubricant' you have added, does right away with any scrappiness. It all flows, one out of another perfectly. If you had 'written up' the stuff, as Kipling would do, you would have ruined it. The phrasing is perfect: often most original. That chapter — 'The Funeral' is magnificent as writing. You have found the word. It knocks one endways. I dont speak of the early chapters i-xv — because I want to reread them — but you wind into your subject with an uncanny art. Chaps 4-10 — go on deepening & deepening, as the recruits sink deeper into R.A.F. mud. The feeling of the Hut & Fatigue life, sweeping out of existence all former states of consciousness rivets one horribly — & the sensations of the breathless struggle with time, to get things done in time, is nightmarish. The Cadet College comes as a relief to the blackness — & it's also admirably written; but you grow a little sententious in your Airman propaganda. Yes, that's overdone a trifle. I don't mind that because luckily it dries up: & you wind up with three fine, last chapters, fine in their ease & naturalness. Well, you've done it, now! I don't advise you ever to write 'a book'. A man who can write 'Funeral' — can write anything — whenever he pleases: — whether he takes 'notes' or doesn't. He's only got to write tersely of what he sees & feels & there it is. I told you, how many times? before.

I shall have a typewritten copy or two made at once./I'm not going to send the original MS to Trenchard. (He would have a motor smash, & the book would be burnt in the smash. 'Awfully Sorry'.) The 'Mint' will frighten him & most people horribly. Then I shall advise Cape to make you an offer for it. — not a word to be altered. He will probably take my advice. Then things will rest I suppose, à la-The Seven Pillars, till you make up your mind. There will be Alarums in High Quarters — & in your own High Quarters, & your spiritual low quarters also. David will read the MS, & write you I suppose, in about a fortnight. I haven't exhausted the subject in any sense — but now I'll remain your exultant & 'told you so' critic

Edward Garnett

Yes by God, its extreme naturalness & concise simplicity & frankness make it a masterpiece.

Answered by D.G. 359

[1] *Acknowledging receipt of* The Mint *manuscript;* cf. D.G. 353.

Cf. D.G. 356, *written at Karachi on the previous day*

3.v.28   19, Pond Place, sw3

I got your cable on Monday & will, of course, only lend the MS of 'The Mint' to 'Trenchard & others', & not the typescript.

The Marsh-Trenchard lunch was amusing. Trenchard is clever & laid all his cards on the table. He is afraid of anything you write, being used against the Air Force, & said he would fight against its publication to the last. He produced several of your letters to him & his letter to you which elicited your cable to him — 'publication impossible. I hold the copyright'. I said of course that 'The Mint' would not harm the Air Force, but he said he was the Air Force, & the Air Force was him & that many powerful enemies were plotting its disruption, etc. etc. He seems rather proud of the conditions you describe in Part I & even of the Commandant's régime, — which curiously enough he introduced into his talk — he had heard the 'other side', & said your smile had infuriated him! I think Trenchard anticipates pretty accurately the contents of 'The Mint'. He further gave me his view of you: & of the circumstances of your leaving the R.A.F. — which he said had nothing to do with the Daily Express business, or with Sir Samuel Hoare, — & altogether he was most informative. His face seemed to me precisely indicative of his mind. I liked him on the whole, but I should not care to be under him. He might sit for a picture of Mars. But then your feminine side has a passion for being under these heavy military men. Trenchard is one of the innumerable types of fighting men who are glorifyed by your clean young privates.

I arranged to send T 'The Mint' MS when I have got a typescript. David's wife is slowly typing the Mint, — so T wont get it yet awhile. Then I suppose Cape will make you a formal offer for, say, so many hundred Privately Printed copies at so much — which offer you will reject, & there I suppose the matter will rest till you or Trenchard die. I said indeed to T. that 'the death of you or of Lawrence seems to be the best chance for the book' — but I fancy that he thinks that you are like the cat with nine lives — & he replied with another anecdote of you.

EG.

17.v.28   19, Pond Place, Chelsea, sw3

Yours of April 23 has reached me, & you will have received by now my letter of the 20th about The Mint. And my letter of May 3, about my interview with Trenchard will be in your hands, unless it was consumed in the fire on a mail train in Egypt, of which we read.

I shall send the Mint (MS) to Trenchard next week. He is keen to read it — but David's typist has been long on the job — & David has been correcting the errors in typescript. I will send you a copy presently. I knew that The Mint would be a work of art, (not 'the notes' you spoke of). And that's why the effect is so craftsmanlike. All you say about the processes of writing it are those of an artistic creation. Of course Trenchard hasn't the faintest idea of what a 'work of art' implies. He thinks that you simply 'put it all down'. But he is shrewd enough over other matters.

Well you've done something 'very good' in the Mint. I told Trenchard it would survive the R.A.F: but I don't think he grasped the idea at all.

I suppose this note will reach you in your new abode, & that you will have sent me your address. But possibly the Gods have other aims than your going 'up country'.

EG.

29.v.28   19, Pond Place, Chelsea, sw3

Just a line in reply to your Tolstoyan letter of May 2. Your injunctions shall be followed rigorously. A typescript has been sent to your brother. And David's copy & mine shall be locked away both in the safe & the recesses of our literary consciences. You want however, you say, Cape to 'reject' the book. But its no use offering it him, if you bar publication till 1950! Also if people are not to talk of it as a book in that case G.B.S mustn't see it — as it will suit his reforming — hold-forth to the world spirit, alarmingly: he might blow up the Services generally with it as the instrument. The 'Sackcloth & ashes' policy you outline does credit to your puritanical complex.

I have just sent off the original MS to Trenchard. You are right in thinking it will lie heavy on his stomach; but that he may not even read the whole I doubt. He is too scared to neglect doing so & of course <u>he</u> may have it typewritten for his private consumption by a trusty hand. I wonder!

It got David rather badly — & after his wife had read it, you, the idol, fell off your pedestal, but was picked up quickly & wiped & replaced there. She explained <u>why</u> you had fallen, but as it was half right and half wrong her criticisms of you, I spare the details.

I think you underestimate 'My Heart & My Flesh'[1] — but I must read it again.

I go to Bantry, Co Cork for a fortnight, tomorrow & will write you from there.

EG.

[1] *By Elizabeth Madox Roberts. T.E.L. had criticized it as* Admirable, but too anxious: too dry: a little 'Steinish' (D.G. 356).

[*mid-August* 1933]   C/o F. Baker Esq, Boscean Cottage,
St Just, Cornwall

Your letter finds me here on holiday.

I was glad to get it, & know that I have a place with the veterans of Hogarth's company in your feeling. It is a high honour. Miss Heath has frightened me so with tales of incompetent packers, that I will leave the Allenby at 2, Smith Square[1] on my return & throw the responsibility for transporting it on to you. A's expression in the eyes is dominating. And this reminds me that I want you to come & look at a portrait of myself by Joan Manning-Sanders. She goes very deep & has contrived to catch me as a Critic — my Critical Quiddity as Charles Lamb would put it. It is remarkably searching, though the ladies think that it might be more beautiful! I have other portraits by Joan, all rather remarkable.

When you speak of yourself — 'all the best in me has gone out & the endurance tougher than other men's' — you have no doubt reached the dividing line in the forties, when most men find a sudden drop in their powers, & in their spring of energy. But if you husband your powers, & dont squander the hours for rest & sleep, you will build yourself up again, & regain a good deal of your forces. There is a regular diminution in the scale of energy at 40, at 50 & again at 60, & 70. But you go on, on the level, so to say for each successive ten years. Only take things as quietly as you can do now for the next ten years, & avoid overtaxing yourself in any way. I have little endurance, nervously & by 'giving out' quickly, I have preserved my health by putting little strain on myself. But of course one is killed by the flaw in some organ increasing Thus Hogarth's heart gave out, & so with the lungs or kidneys or bowels — and is suddenly smitten in one of them. I have just been reading in Montaigne how his father had

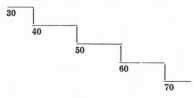

never suffered a day's illness till he was 67, when a great stone developed in his bladder which tormented him the rest of his life. I have just perused Cotton's translation of M — which do you prefer? By the way Cape said he was sending you 'Capajon' — 54 short stories selected by EG from 24 authors. It certainly represents my taste. I should like to know how the volume strikes you when you have time to judge it. I agree with you that only 'the necessary, the inevitable, the high pressure stuff is worth having'. And that Buchan is nowhere by my standard. But most of the 24 authors I select from are still alive. I admit that they have all done their best work by now, & ought to stop writing. So we join hands on that./

Yes, I find I advised Cape to take McCleish's 'The Conquistadores'. I thought it the real stuff — very fine & strong, though David didn't — he is a bit too narrow & exacting & gets 'put off' unnecessarily. What do you think of De la Mare's 'The Fleeting'? It is full of his peculiar magic, & I am amused by the way he deals out to his readers death, disease, destruction & disillusionment in the first 40 pages.

Cape sent me an MS by Capt Liddell Hart on your record as strategist in the Arabian field, etc. It seemed to me a carefully boiled down summary from 'The Seven Pillars' & the only thing I queried was — the passage about your attitude to your father & his first family. I daresay that you dont disagree with it — but I wondered whether you had passed it. Chapter I was missing. I dont know who your father was. What was his title?

I turned up a Brady pedigree by accident & found that a Brady married a Dutchwoman in 1750, & a Potts married a Dutchwoman earlier, so we can claim mysterious affinities there, though I wish I had some Scandinavian blood, like yours, to harden me. The Garnetts, again married an Irishwoman, a Butler of Kilkenny, in the 18th century, so we both have a fine mixed brew.

Yes you put that well about the Irishmen being disappointing men, when you say 'They go so far magnificently & cease to grow. They bring forth more promise and less fruition than the rest of the English world massed against them'.

They have no sense of architecture, & they wont take enough

pains to be artists. O'Faolain has just written a novel, for example, 'A Nest of Simple Folk' which starts off magnificently & then declines into a mere chronicle of family life in Limerick & Cork. It's unusual, & real & has much quality: but compared with what it ought to be & might have been; its a damned piece of Irish evasiveness. He has no faith in life, as the best men have, as you have & I have — to make a declaration — not that I should call my feeling faith, but rather belief. However this is d — d commonplace stuff.

Yours
EG.

Yes, you must really rest. And I'm sorry to hear that you have 18 months of R.A.F service before you. You've surely done more than your share for the flying soldiers.

Answered by D.G. 499

[1] *A pastel portrait by Eric Kennington, given by Garnett to T.E.L. (D.G. 299 and 499): 2 Smith Square, Westminster, was Sir Herbert Baker's house.*

HARLEY GRANVILLE-BARKER
1877-1946

Printed heading

6.xii.23   Connaught Hotel, Mayfair, w1

My dear Shaw
            Not gone, but on the hop. First to Paris, where'll we'll be a week at least
                Hotel Lotti
                rue Castiglione

(oddly enough i.e. a grim appropriateness if your book[1] arrives there — as I hope — it was Mark Sykes' ending place).[2] I do — we both do — badly want to read your book in any form 350,000-550,000 words, if you like. I'm pretty sure it will travel safely to me — book post, registered or other; not <u>parcel</u>, is my only warning.

Your 'argument' on my retirement was a fair retort. And I welcomed it, partly that I might explain to some one who might care to know, whom I cared should know that it wasn't planless. As it happens inclination does combine with what I think is wisdom to do a few years spade-work — it'll be wintry for a while yet.

But even more I welcomed it as it helped towards friendly speaking with you, which I'd wanted after hearing you just one minute.

You have a 'Daimon' (we all have when we've any surplus of vitality at all) — and he'll call on you again when you have accumulated enough power. And you need a lot, your 'game' takes a world wider sweep than does mine.

And as for your feelings about what's done: well, I suppose, your religious biologist would say that this whole world has been built up on a series of well-intentioned mistakes; it being the intention that persists and survives. For further insight into which consideration see Vol III Sc 2 of The Secret Life

Well, we do look forward to the book (Don't forget either to pass our names to your banker friend!)[3] and to seeing you again in the Spring.

Yours
Harley Granville-Barker

[1] *The 'Oxford' printed draft of* Seven Pillars.
[2] *Sir Mark Sykes, who, on behalf of the British Government, made a secret agreement with France to partition the Arab countries; he committed suicide.*
[3] *As subscribers to the limited edition of* Seven Pillars.

Upon receipt of the privately-printed Letters from T. E.
Shaw to Bruce Rogers (1933) *about the translation of the*
Odyssey.

Printed heading

9.vii.33   18, Place Des Etats-Unis, XVIe. Kléber 41-38

My dear T.E.S
    I like to have the little book, and thank you: the
little parasitic flea — but why should I also not drop into poetry
I like to have this little flea
Picked from the noble carcase of your Odyssey — not far, not
farther!!
Flea or louse — you may have your choice: whether it displays
you as morally agile as the one or as coy to searchers as the other.
But here is a chastening reflection: I read through those letters
with more interest than most works of literary art would rouse in
me. The bar of soap metaphor does not hold for literary art — try
it with a poem or a play! But perhaps that is what is wrong with
literary art — See Tolstoy, passion. Too late for me to be saved
however. I must go down to hell, an artist!
    When do you get discharged? Then may see you. I begin to
think you may have shown a wise prescience when you took
refuge in the R.A.F. God knows, I never thought much of the
world as it was. Except for sentiment. I don't regret its break up.
But am one of a generation which can only be a drag on the coach
to prevent it running down hill too fast. You may live to help tug
it up the next hill, having conserved your strength; and that's
exhilarating. I shan't. Yes, and you have apprenticed yourself to
a machine, also. I fly now — by Imperial Airways; helplessly.
But it doesn't seem a bit strange.

                                        Yours
                                        HGB

What's your address?

ROBERT GRAVES
1895-

For the other side of the correspondence see T. E. Lawrence
to his Biographer Robert Graves — *cited below as* R.G.

[?*Feb.* 1922]

O, you!

Ex-diplomat now?

In a week's time we are ready for you if you'll come. Nancy &
child marvellously well.

Did you know that Ecclesiasticus is full of Meleager & has
therefore been accused of being an Alexandrian? Another Gada-
rene, eh?

Life is restored to its usual colour; who'd be an Odysseus but for
the thought of Penelope, however much of a Tough she appears
to the gentry of Ithaca?

Cortez & Pizarro had an awfully easy job compared with your
Arabian problem; they started as a legend and had only to swash a
few buckles and there they were — But to start as a suspect
member of a despised culture as you did, that's a different show;
& the psychology is far more interesting than the obvious reactions of Aztecs & Peruvians. That is for your book to expand.
And I can't imagine how it isn't going to be Literature anyhow.
But also it seems to me that as its a story that can't be published
in your lifetime because it will hamper you so in your future
operations whatever they may be; so, if you have not yet done this,
it would seem to be a necessary step to take one of your linotype
copies for nobody in the world to see till 2022 [at which date a
long erotic poem (not fleshly in the Ross sense but frankly
erotic) of mine appears] and on it work out the personal reasons
contained in the preface, in relation to the text. That would
inevitably make it the most magnificent book ever written.
Happy 2022! Well?   R.G   But don't answer.

About No Decency Left (1932) *by Barbara Rich, a pen-name for Robert Graves and Laura Riding. T.E.L. had contributed a description of an autogiro of the future (pp.* 153-5, *quoted* R.G. *pp.* 168-9)

[*Spring* 1932]

T.E.

That novel. It was sent off to Cape last week. It is strictly anonymous & it was not written by me. That is, I wrote it and rewrote it & had it typed & then Laura saw it & it wasn't good enough and she rewrote it with/for me and made quite a different thing of it. Made it what it should originally have been. I shall send you a proof. Please mark anything that I got wrong in putting your autogiro in. Please also say if any objection to joking mention of your name as a celebrated British spy (by the Lyonesse Communist leader) And if you notice any grave error in procedure anywhere.

Remember me to speed-boats. We sent you To Whom Else. Acknowledge at leisure. You are constantly in my mind particularly today when I have a letter about the German edition of Lawrence & the Arabs. Had quite forgotten the book.

Laura sends her greetings. We arent coming to England until Jan, I'm afraid.

R.G.

In further reply to letter of July 30th, 1933 (R.G. *p.* 172)

[*Autumn* 1933]   Canellun, Deyá, Mallorca, Spain

Dear T.E.

I wrote in answer to your very decent letter. Did you get it? I don't want you to think that I didn't answer at once. I wrote to Cloud's Hill.

In the letter I said amongst other things that I would like you to read my Claudius book in proof. Will you? The proofs will be obtainable by now from Arthur Barker (21 Garrick St, Covent Garden) if you send for them. Any scholarly comment such as that so-and-so would not have gone in a litter but on foot to this or that function or that Roman houses had no balconies and onions weren't invented etc etc would be welcome. I don't know the geography of Rome at first hand & my maps I have worked from aren't clear. I don't want any too great howlers. The book is largely guess-work & imagination but I want it to hold water & have done a great deal of reading to get it passable. Could you do this for me, possibly, & do it at once? And send page-references to me here?

Robert

Excuse messy letter. My eyes have gone bad on me & I economise on fair copies.

Obviously your best way to earn money for your house-debts[1] is to go to some big immoral publisher like [*name omitted*] or [*name omitted*] and say: 'you may put my name on the list of your directors on payment of a fee of £1000 a year. I shall be ready to advise you about books and help you to get promising authors, but I shall not bind myself to hours of work or office routine.' They'd jump at it. Even a small, not immoral publisher would accept. If youre too shy to do it I know how to do it for you without compromising either of us.

[1] *T.E.L. had written on July 30th:* 'The dollar fell, and the crisis stopped all American book-sales. So a third of the translation's royalty will not meet the builder's bills [*for improving Clouds Hill*]. Robin Buxton, who is still my banker, has come to the rescue with an overdraft: but now prophesy to me ... Will books revive in the States, or am I stuck for good? I deprecate an English reprint of the Odyssey — nor is there money, here, in new versions of the classics (R.G. *p.* 173).

In reply to letter of November 12th, 1933, criticizing his I, Claudius (R.G. p. 174). The second of a pair of undated letters from Mallorca

[*Nov. or Dec.* 1933]

Second Letter

T.E,

I was just about to post the other letter when yours came, and as I like answering every point in a letter before it gets stale I tore open the envelope to insert this. Your remarks are of two kinds, those about Claudius & those about me and I shall answer them separately. First about Claudius. Assegai is from French azagaye, via Portuguese from orig. Arab-Berber az-zaghāyah. First use in English recorded 1625 (N.E.D.) but I saw a letter in Times Litt. Sup. about a year or two ago giving 14th century quotation. Assegai be damned — said enough about it.

I used 'paper' for 'papyrus': I thought that was clear. (authority N.E.D. Late middle English) I also mentioned parchment, in the Livilla-Sejanus context, as a cheaper material and referred to the frequent use of wax-tablets.

The vine-stems of the centurions were used by the mutineers to beat them to death with. 'Shoots' is a mistranslation. I would not like to be beaten with a vine stem. They are as tough & pliant as rawhide almost.

About the crime: yes, its a crime story. But the facts are unescapable and I have at least made Postumus a decent fellow against the prejudice of Tacitus, Suetonius etc, and Germanicus & Agrippina, and Acte and Calpurnia the hetairai (the first invented the second a shadow figure) & Medullina Camilla, and Cocceius Nerva and Drusus Senior and Nero Senior and there are others. I have white- rather than black-washed. And then there is Claudius himself — surely he's a good specimen? — not to mention Cassius Chaerea, and Gallus. I liked Gallus. Tacitus hated him.

About the middle part dragging. I purposely slowed down the

writing in the later Tiberius period because it was necessary for a fuller appreciation of Caligula's insane liveliness. It makes Caligula 'quite a relief' instead of 'such a monster.' It drags but one is kept going by interest in the fate of the few surviving decent characters and a premonition of the old He Goat's sticky end.

Next, remarks about me & Claudius. 'I, Claudius is not an essential book.' Did I say it was? 'I can't say why, exactly, but I feel unsatisfied.' You read it looking for things that I had no intention of putting into it. I chose Claudius for a number of reasons: the first was that he was a historian before he was anything else and because he lived in an age in which every moral safeguard of a religious or patriotic or social sort had gone West — things were just disintegrating. He realized this and found it impossible to reintegrate them. The best he could do was to be a historian & keep historian's faith. The more he tried, as Emperor, to interfere with the process of disintegration the madder things got. But that's for the sequel. Claudius hadn't the courage to give up, as Nerva did; his naive optimism & curiosity kept him going. Well, it all fell to pieces in the end & there was a new, false reintegration with Christianity. That's the point. I prefer Claudius's post-Augustanism to your post-mediaevalism. What you're really saying is 'This is not an idealistic, hopeful book and it isn't even a portrait of a heroic "minority" character resisting tyranny bravely: Claudius is no Brutus.' No, indeed he wasn't. But you and your Englishry ought at any rate to have the greatest respect & sympathy for Claudius as the first Romanizer of Britain. I wrote the most popular book I could write while keeping within the limits of personal integrity: that is, Claudius is an old story but I identify myself with him as much as with any other historical character I know about, even including Skelton. I identify myself with him historically, but merely historically. That was what leaves you unsatisfied. You expect me to write God knows what Golden-Falcon-Book-of-Talbot-up Guards-&-at-'em-Song-of-Solomon stuff & you have no right to expect. I agree it is a pity that Claudius books have to be written because people won't pay a living wage for the essential works, but at present it is so. The essential work is always, of course, going on.

Claudius is only the most stupid side-activity, like eating and dressing & going up & down stairs for fire-wood for the stove. It takes time from the essential work, but not much.

My Englishry was never more than my affection for the English temper and for the English language. These I keep. As for the Mallorcans, especially in the olive-growing parts of the island, they are the least foreign, most immediately intimate people I have ever met. They are in many ways more English than the English and have about the same proportion of blue eyes and fair skins, and sometimes an English intonation.

But what beats me in your letter is your suggestion that I should come 'home' at least for a while & meet people who don't care enormously about my 'subjects' (Roman history do you mean?) and don't value my work: what sort of picture have you of my life here? Do you imagine me surrounded by an adoring band of literary admirers? What would I be likely to meet in England?

No I don't think you Victorian, but you place yourself as an Edwardian in your literary vocabulary — Edward VII, reaching back longingly to Edward I — and you oughtn't to involve me in superb's and masterly's. The writing is definitely not high-pitched but the sort of writing to be expected from the man we know Claudius was. It is a very modest book, & full of anecdotes because people like anecdotes; and the only, to me, really horrible thing is Tiberius's striking out Agrippina's eye. I can't help feeling bad about that, but after all, that was what happened & she & Tiberius can't be cut out of the story.

The book will be valued if it is valued, because it is a good crime story. That is not a 'wrong reason.' People are today predominantly interested in crime. The essential work that is being done here by Laura, a few others & myself takes in the subject of crime and explains why people are now so interested in it. But you are not really interested in the essential work, as you have made perfectly plain, so you have no right to feel unsatisfied with Claudius.

I read a quotation from something you wrote for a Legion publication:[1] I think it is a quite legitimate activity for you to write recruiting propaganda for the Air Force; which probably needs a lot of enlarging against German air activities but you ought to write either quite simply, in the ingenuous vocabulary of a mechanic, the sort you recently recommended to us or disingenuously in the commercially-tainted language of Government advertisement writers — Wembley or Empire-Marketing-Board stuff would provide a model — and not in the language of Lawrence of Jesus College and the near East. Something about narrowing fields in order to reap them with propellers beaten into pruning-hooks and then winnow them with spears* beaten into propellers — wasn't it?

This is a long letter and the situation between us is unsatisfactory. Perhaps it will improve when you become your own master, so long as you don't transfer your vassalage to any other, less benignant, overlordship than the R.A.F — for instance, Literature in the Edwardian sense. And it might improve things if you left 'home' for a time at least & came here.

R.G

* assegais?

1 *The* British Legion Journal *had inadvertently published a mangled extract from* The Mint.

[? *Dec.* 1933]

T.E,
Thank you very much indeed for reading proofs of Claudius, and several points you raised I have settled. About France & assegai. After a lot of thought I decided after all to keep them in but to make an explanation and justification in the preliminary note: which I enclose. You were right about the 200 miles being too short from Pavia to the Waal. My Classical dictionary was wrong. I have put that right & rewritten the passage. (Oh, but first about assegai, a point I haven't made in the note. Tchaka the Zulu introduced the short heavy-headed stabbing assegai as an improvement on the Ama-Zulu practice of breaking the shaft of the missile weapon.)

I have changed Edelstein to Adelstan and Minos's men roasting to breaking on an eternal wheel. I have cut out platoon, though its a good seventeenth-century word, and changed to 'company'.

Hesiod is associated with the 11th Olympiad (735 B.C.) so 700 years is all right. An amusing thing is your query of Augustus's unAugustan speech — it is literally what he said (Dio Cassius). I am hoping that a lot of critics will chance their arm in this sort of comment and fail to distinguish history from my invention.

[*The rest omitted*]

Robert

[1935]   Canellun, Deyá, Mallorca, Spain

Dear T.E.

I wrote to you at Cloud's Hill the same day as you wrote to me here: you will have got my letter, I hope. You answer me one question that I asked, about your cottage etc. I am so sorry that your reserve has fallen so low. 20/- a week is comfortable living in Majorca but very little indeed in England whatever your capacity for going without. I should very much like to bring your income back to £2.2/ for a year or so: may I? I don't think you'll refuse me that. I could find the money in March when I begin to cash in on Claudius: so far I have been 'riding on dead horses' & only just keeping pace with debt. By the end of the summer I expect to be quite unencumbered again: it has been a rotten two years in that way and at one time I thought I was sunk altogether. My mother has been supporting my children meanwhile. A great help has been Korda's decision to do a Claudius film. (Funny, he didn't know about my book about you & I think he'll find it useful in the film he's doing: it's better for studio purposes than Liddell Hart & handier than the 7 Pillars. I told him that there's no copyright in it.)

Your mouse-eyed woman is a liar. Nobody points me out as a sight in Palma. She must have mistaken me for the Prince of Wales, the late Cecil Aldin, Douglas Fairbanks jun or sen, or Mayor Jimmy Walker of New York who has all been seen in Palma lately.

I am sorry you have to leave the R.A.F. because you suited it & it you; but it has probably done its job of slowing you down — I only hope not too well. I

[End of page; the rest is missing]

D. G. HOGARTH
1862-1927
(Then Keeper of the Ashmolean Museum)

About an invitation to visit Lord Carnarvon, father of the Hon. Aubrey Herbert, M.P., to meet Stamboliski, the Bulgarian Prime Minister and representative at the Peace Conference (who signed the Treaty with the Allies on November 27th)

Card   Printed heading

[mid-Nov. 1919]   Ashmolean Museum, Oxford

Just got your proof — I'll read this evening.

Look here — Carnarvon has got Stambolinski & full 'Suite' — probably, I expect, others also to meet them e.g. no doubt, Aubrey & other pro-Bulgars. I'm inclined to cry off by wire — What do you say? Could you go next weekend? i.e. 23rd? Let me know by telephone, unless you can come round. I shan't be in till after dinner.

DGH.

About a Roman inscription at Qaṣr al ʿAzraq, and about means towards relieving the poverty of C. M. Doughty; cf. the letters from Doughty

Postcard   *Printed heading*

28.ii.22   Ashmolean Museum, Oxford

So far as I can make out that Azrak stone has not been published to date; but of course Jaussen may have it. The Emperors shld. be Diocletian & Maximian — & the Latin seems to read (dedication to one Empr. only):

Invicto [*name*]. Pro salute et vict[oria] Impp.
     et Ca[ess.?] Joviorum et Herculiorum.

I can't make out the Greek from that photo, but suspect it of being a d — d metrical thing!

By the way, will you let me know exactly what R.Lit. Fund proposes to do & if it is to be done promptly. I'll write to Yates Thompson (if it is to be R.G.S.) & to Guillemard (to get something out of Cambridge) & I'll suggest other names to you.

DGH.

In reply to a suggestion, made in D.G. 320, *that his* Life of Charles M. Doughty *should compare a series of passages in* Travels in Arabia Deserta *with the notes Doughty had written on the spot*

Printed heading

18.ix.27   20, St. Giles', Oxford

My dear T.E.
[*A paragraph omitted*]
As to C.M.D. I fear I can't over-weight more what is to be not a critical study of his works, but a Memoir of his life.

I've shown a good deal of the process by which A D. grew, &
quoted freely from the Notebooks; but, though I agree about the
interest, I can't do the parallel page business. To be really useful
it would entail, for example, some three or four pages to one of
the Notebook; & that not once or twice but several times, if
the thing were to be any use.

The great difficulty is to read the Notebooks at all & retain any
eyesight! I tried getting pages copied by others, but found that I
had to go all over it again to correct their mistakes. That's the
practical difficulty! No one, not even Mrs. D. can make as much
out of 'em as I, though my eyes are not what they were — So
don't expect very much light. You'll get some!

[*A paragraph omitted*]

Yrs.
DGH.

AUGUSTUS JOHN
1878-1961
return to 28 Mallord St. tomorrow

29.ix.[19]   Dorset

Dear Lawrence,
        I hear Feisal is or is going to be in London. Couldnt
we take him out & give him a feed? Also let me get that drawing
done.

How would it be to continue that portrait of you which some
of the Tait Gallery people dont seem to want?

What are you doing?

Yrs
Augustus John
I have a gorgeous thing to tell you about a portrait lately done
of an ex-grocer & peer. I actually frightened him into violence.[1]

---

[1] *Lord Leverhulme had cut the head out of the portrait.*

Thursday [1920]   28, Mallord St., Chelsea

Dear Lawrence,

Its a good thing to know my Feisal wears well. I'm
very glad. Why was he beaten by the French — because you were
not at his side?

Your Arab gown has come back cleaned.

I will come to Oxford under your auspices. But I know the
place wont suit me.

When you come to town, come & sit again for the drawing.

Yrs.
Augustus John

Printed heading

Hotel-Restaurant de la Tour Eiffel,
1, Percy Street, Tottenham Court Road, Londres, w1

Dear Lawrence,

Since you're doing nothing why not come to Spain
with me to-morrow? I tried to ring you up to-day. Our train
leaves at 11.A.M. Victoria If you cant come to-morrow you can
find me & rescue me in Paris c/o Thomas Earp
56 Avenue de Neuilly
Neuilly-Sur-Seine
where I shall probably be for a day or two — or at any rate heard
of.

Do come

Yrs
John

And we'll do the drawing.

118

28.xi.30   28, Mallord Street, Chelsea, Flaxman 6257

Dear Shaw,

I am glad to hear from you as I couldnt remember your address & wanted to write for long.

As you see I'm in the City of Dreadful Night but expect to go to Fryern soon when I'll let you know. Of course you may take the study and I do want to finish the bigger one.

I've been away in Ireland etc. for ages. I also went to Amsterdam & Paris — to the former place to see a very fine show of pictures — to the latter to make a drawing or two of James Joyce. His mug is largely occluded by several pairs of powerful lenses. Some of his musical friends are making a book in his honour — setting his quite unsingable 'Pomes' to music and I contribute a drawing.

I see somebody else has forestalled you with a life of Casement. His execution seems to have been a very foul bit of work. I read you have been up to mischief with the Bolshies apart from your Kurdistan machination.

Did you read Lewis' latest tome 'The Apes of God'?

Yrs ever
Augustus John

Friday [1935]   Fryern

Dear Shaw,

Just back from a Cornish jaunt. Thanks for the collotypes,[1] they are excellent. Say, you can sure hustle!

I had an idea that that excellent man Emery Walker was dead. Glad I'm wrong.

I hear a report that you are the son of G.B.S. If so he should

119

have repeated the effort. (I mean this kindly.) ... [*Two sentences follow: see reproduction on facing page*]

Yrs ever
Aug. John

[1] *Reproductions of his last drawing of T.E.L.; they were made by Emery Walker, for the frontispiece of a projected edition of* The Mint (cf. D.G. 554).

RUDYARD KIPLING
1865-1936

About raising support for a proposal to establish an American Mandate over Syria, cf. D.G. 111 et seq.

Printed heading

7.i.19   Bateman's, Burwash, Sussex

<u>private</u>

Dear Lawrence.

I wanted very much to get a word with you after we met at Doubleday's[1] rooms — about your U.S. Asia notion: and to tell you that the only American who could visualize it was Theodore Roosevelt. Today (we being shadows) he is dead & the loss on all counts is not to be reckoned.

But my meaning is that it is to the Republicans — not to the Democrats now in a minority in both Senate and Congress — that you must look for the furtherance of your idea. Wilson's most human and most politic notion is to give lofty advice and return to his national fireside: and the men he has appointed — such as Davies Ambassador[2] are, most like, of the same mind — against taking 'responsibilities' in the face of a critical world.

Fryern.   Friday

Dear Shaw, 'Just back from a Cornish
taunt. Thankly for the Collotypes, they are
excellent. Say, you can sure hustle!
had an idea that that excellent man
Emery Walker was dead. Glad I'm wrong.
I hear a report that you are the son
of G.B.S. If so he should have repeated
the effort. (I mean this kindly)
If we had had a bit more time you have
done some more fashion plates. not that
I dont like this one which is quite trim.
Hope to be about in March when you return
to freedom.
                Yrs ever, Augs. John

[actual size]

Oct. 8. 1919.

[actual size]
see page 122

Dear Lawrence

Naturally, if you didn't take what was offered you and do what you were wanted to do, you would — from the F. O. point of view — be the worst kind of crook. They don't understand deviations from type. Later on, I expect, you will be accused of having been actuated by "provincial motives" in all you did. Wait till you are cussed for being a "venal hireling" — as I was once — in a legislature.

But we are all sitting in the middle of wrecked hope and broken dreams. I tried all I knew to put the proper presentation of the American scheme before men over there who, I thought, would help but one can't expect people whose forbears went West to avoid trouble to stand up to responsibility in a far land for no immediate cash return.

[...] of the game — [...] minute to stop [...] young, and [...] large on "old, [...] ails" and a bit of a [...]

[...] these things and [...] in town. [...] urge to come [...] next week? [...] course, and [...] be down with [...] Tunbridge in the morning (you x usually get a lot of arrears) then we can [...] have a talk with me (which please bring there and all) we'll here for some time and any time next week will suit. If you will write your train the car will meet you at Etchingham and we'd all be delighted. DO see if you can fix it

Ever yours
Rudyard Kipling

P.S. I think the cinema man is the last + most perfect touch of foolishness. What a lot Dante missed in his Inferno by not keeping abreast with "modern progress"!

But (you probably know all this) a good many Republicans have come over to keep watch on Wilson. I don't know their names but you will, and Davies' ear is to the ground to learn what these men are doing. That being always an Ambassador's first job. Incidentally Doubleday is in the Wilson interest, though friendly to Roosevelt. It might serve your plans were you to approach these Republicans if — which I believe to be the case — the star of Wilson is on the wane.

I have lived for years in the U.S.A. and though I have not been back for a long time I have a large circle of American correspondents. I had a very full letter from Roosevelt only last week and I know from that the drift of what the Republicans meant to do, under his guidance, in Senate & Congress when they come in, with their majority, in March. Remember that then will be the first time that Wilson will be subjected to any political pressure from the Opposition. Cabot Lodge — an old man unluckily — but always in charge of foreign affairs in the Senate — is one of the most important men now to be considered in the U.S.A. This at least is how it seems to me. What says the perspicuous Lebid?[3]

> Strangers at the Kings Court come thirsting for booty ...
> Our fathers held power as it came from their fathers
> We give Law to the Nations, our promises bind us
> And what God hath given us we deal it equally

Ever sincerely
Rudyard Kipling

---

[1] *F. N. Doubleday, the American publisher.*
[2] *John W. Davis, then American Ambassador in London.*
[3] *An Arab poet, contemporary with Mohammed.*

8.x.19   Bateman's, Burwash, Sussex

Dear Lawrence

Naturally, if you didn't take what was offered you and do what you were wanted to do, you would — from the F.O. point of view — be the worst kind of crook. They don't understand deviations from type. Later on, I expect, you will be accused of having been actuated by 'financial motives' in all you did. Wait till you are cussed for being a 'venal hireling' — as I was once — in a Legislature.

But we are all sitting in the middle of wrecked hope and broken dreams. I tried all I knew to put the proper presentation of the American scheme before men over there who, I thought, would help. But one can't expect people whose forbears went West to avoid trouble to stand up to responsibility in a far land for no immediate cash return.

But you will not go out of the game — except for the necessary minute to step aside and vomit. You are young, and the bulk of the men now in charge are 'old, cold and of intolerable entrails' and a lot of 'em will be dropping out soon.

But it's impossible to write these things and it's hopeless to try in talk in town. Do you think you could manage to come down for a night or two next week? There will be no one here of course, and you'd better bring some work down with you, because I'm at the grindstone in the morning. (You've probably got a lot of arrears). Then we can have a talk with maps, which please bring. Mine are old. We're here for some time and any time next week would suit. If you will write your train the car will meet you at Etchingham and we'd all be delighted. Do see if you can fix it.

Ever yours
Rudyard Kipling

P.S. I think the cinema now is the last & most perfect touch of beastliness. What a lot Dante missed in his Inferno by not being abreast with 'modern progress'.

Typed

Bateman's, Burwash

<u>private</u>

Dear Lawrence,

It looks to me, from your letter of the 20th, as if you had been on the job of that book too long. One gets stale and doubtful in such cases.

However, if you care to trust me with a copy of the work, I will go through it and tell you honestly what I think of it. I do not hold with showing one's friends what one is doing till it is all done, and I very much hope that, as you say, you will not take any advice that I give. My only concern is that the book should be written by you, and, in due time, got out. I may as well warn you that, if you are a pro-Yid, and think that the present cheap Hell in Palestine is 'statesmanship', I shall most likely turn the whole thing back on your hands and refuse to touch it ...

With this reservation, I am all at your service. Only don't tell any one about it.

Ever sincerely yours,
Rudyard Kipling

Printed heading

25.vii.22   Bateman's, Burwash, Sussex

<u>private</u>

Dear Lawrence,

I am not a very communicative animal myself, and, of course have said nothing about it. In return I want you not to tell anyone that you have sent the book to me. It will be better that way.

123

I dare say the French are pigs from certain points of view, but seldom has a race been 'carted', to the extent that we and the U.S. 'carted' them.

Ever sincerely
Rudyard Kipling

SIR GEORGE LLOYD
afterwards Lord Lloyd
1879-1941
(*Then Governor of Bombay*)

Crest   *Printed heading*

Governor of Bombay, Government House, Ganeshkhind
26.viii.20

<u>Private</u>

My dear T.E.L.
No news of you for so long except through the newspapers — Was there ever so fatal and disastrous a muddle over Egypt Syria, Palestine and Mesopotamia. I am beginning to think that when you and I kept repeating our familiar tags, you 'Alexandretta!' and I 'Gibraltars not territory' were not only saying & meaning the same things but right things — If we had taken & kept the Basra-Kurna bit, & taken & kept Alexandretta & told the Franks that it was not Syria & stuck to that & let the rest rip we should have had the peoples inside all on our side against everyone outside — Now what?
I don't know what to think about Egypt — perhaps its right perhaps its wrong — we all know what happens to Empires when they begin to withdraw their legions; but what I do know is that in India we can't stand this fast bowling from Whitehall. What we have done in Egypt[1] is going to obliterate the reforms here

completely and provoke a passionate cry for independence complete here in this country. 'Our special position in the Nile Valley'!! The Indian will say 'We too recognise your special position on the Afghan frontier — but for the rest, filez!'

And the way Feisal has been treated![2]

I'm too dispirited & anxious to write more —

Yours
G.L.

[1] *The Milner-Zaghlul agreement, just concluded (but never ratified by the British Government), provided that Egypt become independent but undertake certain obligations to meet British interests.*
[2] *The French had expelled Feisal from his kingdom of Syria.*

Crest   Printed heading

Governor of Bombay, Government House, Ganeshkhind
I.X.20

My dear T.E.L.

Thanks for your note and the dewdrop from the Civil Service Probationers — there are not many dewdrops bestowed upon one in this country I can assure you so it came pleasantly. I don't think I ever knew a country in which abuse was so lavishly bestowed in the newspapers as in India — it doesn't matter one bit what you do, its part of a policy to abuse everything done by Government — and I don't know that I mind it much anyway — it makes one yawn sometimes.

P.Z.[1] came through the other day with Mrs P.Z. I think he has got a tough job on, for its a pretty good mess as you say. They will come back to your policy all right, indeed I think they have done so, but perhaps its too late. We shall see.

Jaffer Pasha[2] stayed with me a couple of nights ago — He has lost his beard — Last time I saw him was at Akaba just before he went somewhere Tafile I think — with him Haji Belshah the man who failed to teach me to speak Arabic. Its plaguey hot just now and I wish I had your refreshing company. Just came back from Bombay where I have been trying to raise £6.000.000 to clean up Bombay with — No one in the East ever forgives you for trying to clean them up and I'm not sure they aren't right, but they like me and look upon it as my little fad, are quite confident I shan't really do it, and will give me six million to keep me good & happy.

The Viceroy thinks I shan't get it and is rather sorry for me — You see the Govt. of India loan only got in the whole of India about £4 million of new money — but you can't do it by printed prospectuses — You know how it can, autocracy and jokes in stripes — much the same way as a hamla starts off from Akaba, never on the day you appoint or quite in the way you meant, but if you ride ahead at the right moment everyone comes tumbling along after you in bits and you get there often faster than the serjeant major.

But I mustn't bother you with shop very local, & parochial — I apologise; but so 'the midges hymn,

      'answers the Seraphim'

      'Athwart

      'the Oceans Court'.

Does Thorne[3] ever come & see you?

Yours

GL.

1 *Sir Percy Z. Cox, High Commissioner in the newly-created Mandatory territory of Iraq, was on his way from London to Baghdad with instructions to form a national State.*

2 *Ja'far Pasha al Askari, on his way to Baghdad to become a Minister in the first Government of Iraq.*

3 *A Yeomanry trooper whom Lloyd took with him to Arabia in* 1917 (*see* Seven Pillars).

FREDERIC MANNING
1887-1935

Writing to Robert Graves in 1933, *T.E.L. named Manning first among* the three I most care for, since Hogarth died (D.G. 480)

Embossed heading

7.iii.22   Edenham, Bourne, Lincs.

Dear Lawrence:

Will Rothenstein wrote me that he had heard from you; and told me also of Mr Cape's good opinion and friendliness. I think the best reward of work is in the friends it makes for one; and that you are among them gives me a sense of pride.

If ever you feel like a quiet, not to say lonely, week-end, would you care to come on a visit to me and see my books? At present I am only in temporary quarters, but I can give you a comfortable room, as I have my own furniture. The rest of the house is rather primitive.

In any case, I hope to go up to Town in a few weeks; and perhaps that will give me an opportunity of seeing you again.

Yours always sincerely
Frederic Manning

Embossed heading

31.iii.22   Edenham, Bourne, Lincs.

Dear Lawrence:

I am sorry you can't come. If you had, you would have found me not evolving a proper rhythm of prose, but still digesting official reports, and translating the Jargon of Admiralty documents into a reasonable, if pedestrian, speech.

Come then, after Baghdad. My dreams of the East were shattered long ago, and I recreate them only in reading Mardrus' Mille Nuits et Une Nuit, or his Reine de Saba: both reactions from reality.

You will have the Romances soon, and you will like it as well as Scenes & Portraits. Only I am not really polishing it. I never polish. If a thing doesn't come right at once it goes into the waste paper basket and is re-written. If it does come right correction consists only in omission and an attempt towards greater brevity.

Send me anything from Uruk;[1] and I confess I am anxious to see your own book. You don't head me off by being yourself over-conscientious in the matter of style.

You apply the Epicurean doctrine too literally in concealing your address, but I shall send this to All Souls'.

The benediction of Allah, the omnipotent ... the most merciful, (which should have been prefatory)

Yours sincerely
Frederic Manning

[1] *Antiquities from the Sumerian city, the setting of one of his* Scenes and Portraits (1909).

About his war novel, published anonymously, under his Army number, by Peter Davies (1929) — the full text entitled The Middle Parts of Fortune, *the expurgated version* Her Privates We; *T.E.L. had guessed the authorship by recognizing the style*

Printed heading

11.ii.30   Grand Hotel Panhans, Semmering

My dear Shaw:

Was it some uncanny flair, that led you to me; or did Will Rothenstein tell you that he has some letters from me with my regimental number on them, 19022? I have been rather anxious lest he should discover it; and that indeed was the only reason why I did not send him a copy. Not of The Middle Parts. Peter rationed me too severely for that, but of Her Privates We. Some day I shall.

You praise the book with a magnificent generosity. I was a little afraid of it as I wrote it. It was wilful and spontaneous, and took its own way. It came so hurriedly that some things were forgotten. Peter took it from me sheet by sheet, and cast it into adamantine type. But for him I might have re-written it. What an escape!

I am really very grateful for what you say. I am glad that you and Barrie are moved by it. In another way I am glad that Arnold Bennett wrote as he did about it: about it being a tribute to the men, I mean. I have forgiven him everything for saying that.

If you will be in London between the 21st and 28th I shall be at Garlands Hotel, Suffolk St, Pall Mall. Let me have a line there saying whether you could lunch or dine. I may be in London for about three weeks, but after the 28th my brother's arrival from Australia makes things a little uncertain.

I had your address a couple of years ago from Cherry Garrard of Lammer: but somehow I did not write.

Yours always
Frederic Manning

Answered by D.G. 406

In reply to D.G. 406

Printed heading

14.iii.30   26, Gilbert Street, Brook Street, w1

My dear Shaw:
        I have not been well, or I should have thanked you for your letter before now. I don't know whether I can thank you

for your praises, and support, of my book: it would leave me bankrupt of gratitude. I am a little terrified of the publicity, in which Davies is an adept, and yet I am greedy enough of the praises of my friends. I think the intellectual preoccupations of authorship weakens one's will; and what I used to consider as vanity in other men, I recognize, now, to be only the need to be reassured as to the quality of one's work. You and I know that The Middle Parts of Fortune bears traces of the haste in which it was written; you point out one of its stylistic defects,[1] but tho' I wrote all in a little over six months, it was not hastily conceived: even during the war I thought of writing it: so perhaps the whole is capable of carrying off the defects in some of its parts.

Why do you talk about the dregs of your reputation? All reputation is the dregs of the wine we drink in action, if only in our interior action. Fame is the enduring strength of the action itself, after it has escaped from our hands, and has achieved a separate existence. You communicated an impulse to men, overcoming their inertia, & the action is continuous even after you have ceased to be concerned in it.

I should like to go and see you. Would you like it?

Yours always sincerely
Frederic Manning

[1] *T.E.L. had written:* Just sometimes you seem to mix up the 'one's' and 'his's' (D.G. 406).

T.E.L. wrote on March 21st, 1930 (in answer to the preceding letter): The worst thing about fame, I think, is that in a few years steady experience of it the victim begins to believe it, against the sure and certain knowledge of his own heart. And then he's a living lie. *And his letter of February 25th, 1930, had ended:* What is so dead as a book one has written? (D.G. 406)

26.iii.30   The Bull Inn, Bourne, Lincs.

Dear Shaw:
      When I contrasted fame with reputation I was thinking of it as entirely posthumous. I think all reputation, unless one is a politician, who trades on it, a negligible, because a purely attributive, quality. By repute I am supposed to be many things which I know I am not, so it does not worry me. Yes, praise pleases me, and any blame or offence to my pride hurts damnably for a moment, but I am, almost immediately, indifferent. I like, or dislike people, spontaneously and as Falstaff has it on instinct. I may invent reasons for my likes and dislikes later. After I had spoken to you, or to poor Charles Whibley, for five minutes I felt you were both old friends of mine, and the mere fact that we met rarely or only once, did not affect the feeling. You can't really judge of your own work, any more than I can of mine. You ask me 'What is so dead etc.'? But a book is not dead merely because it has achieved a separate existence and escaped from the control of your own executive will. Your action on it has ceased, and its action on other minds is incomprehensible to you, that's all. I wish I had read your book, but I could neither buy nor borrow it. My chief criticism of the ordinary edition — The Revolt in the Desert — was that from one point of view its quality might seem a defect That quality was its poetry: the heat of poetry consumes its material too completely, a defect in an historical record. I admired it for its poetry: one approached a sentence which seemed as hard and clean as marble, and one looked back on it as on a mirage. I did not want an historical record I was completely satisfied to follow the action of

131

a mind reflecting its past experience and still a little tremulous and excited by it. The characters seemed to me very definite and vivid. I wish I had been able to read it as The Seven Pillars, as I feel even in Her Privates We that bowdlerizing the bad language diminishes the violence of the contrasts in some passages, & that, after all, was only a slight alteration. Your book has a permanent place.

It would be great fun to see you in the summer; and to read your experience as a recruit. I had a bad time, and was <u>not</u> cheerful, during my own training: it woke up my powers of resistance. You will find this a portentous letter, in its length. Anyway forgive its clumsiness; and will you make a note of an address which will always find me

c/o The Australian Bank of Commerce
62, Bishopsgate. E.C.2

I am a nomad. Do you remember you were coming down to read your book to me — and went to Baghdad instead? Then I lived three miles from here.

Yours always
Frederic Manning

Printed heading

14.iv.30   Park Lane Hotel, Piccadilly, London, w1

Dear Shaw:

I should like immensely to read the book: at my ease, as it were, and in slippers. Do you mind sending it to Peter Davies's office? I think that would be the safest address, as I shall be moving about after this week and the Bank invariably writes and asks what to do about any parcel: they only forward letters as a matter of course.

When I have written three pages of a letter I usually find I have forgotten my original intention, and started another hare instead.

I did not expect you to be much excited by Epicurus, but I thought it might amuse you to see it.[1] At a party in Rome about thirteen months ago, an Italian came up to me, and said he had paid a visit to Oxford, where W. D. Ross had recommended him to read my introduction to Epicurus, as it treated him from a new point of view. The novelty consisted in examining the facts given by Cicero, and discarding Cicero's anti-Epicurean tendencies! Any way you should not neglect to read some Greek, or a Latin poet. I dare say you do keep something of the kind about you. On se doit son propre secret! I used to imagine myself completely merged in the men about me, and then find myself miraculously alone, something unassimilable in me asserting itself and filling me with a kind of despair. There is something extraordinarily fascinating in soldiering, even under the most rigorous discipline one feels oneself hors la loi. I am really impatient to read of your experiences as a recruit.

Yours always
Frederic Manning

[1] *He had sent a copy (inscribed* To T. E. Shaw for the purpose of comparison from Frederic Manning. 3.iii.30) *of a book published four years previously,* Epicurus's Morals: collected, and faithfully Englished, by W. Charlton; with an introductory Essay by F. Manning.

Printed heading

14.iv.30   Park Lane Hotel, Piccadilly, London, w1

My dear Shaw:
        I had no sooner posted my letter to you, than one came to me from 'AE' (George Russell) saying: 'Lawrence guessed you. So he must know you. What kind of human being is he? His deeds and writings I know, but I wonder does he know himself. I think him a fascinating fellow, and would like to

133

listen to him talking, to see what kind of spirit is in him.' You
would like him. He is a gentle creature easily amazed at the
unreason of life and yet practical in everything but his thought,
which is all vision.

Yours always
Frederic Manning

Answered by D.G. 413

About Seven Pillars

9.v.30   26, Gilbert Street, Brook Street, w1

Dear Shaw:
    The book is magnificent. I should have written to
you long before now, to acknowledge its arrival and thank you
for it; but having launched myself into it at once, and read it
practically without intermission, I waited until I should have
some leisure in which to write, and in my present ill-regulated
life there is little. Here I can be alone for an hour or two.

It is a magnificent book. Magnificent is the right word, for
your mind spent itself without stint, even prodigally, for a great
occasion. At the same time it is an exceptionally difficult book.
The difficulties of the subject are enormous: the background is
continually dissolving and changing. There is the background of
the desert; the background of the war; the political background,
of the English in Egypt (so alien among those spiritual quick-
sands as to be almost irrelevant), and of the Arab revolt (in itself
so ambiguous, a racial movement striving to assume a national
character, the nomad entering into possessions, arresting his own
movement by prescribing a boundary to it). You took me right
back to Genesis and Job. When you describe the action of the
nomad on the town-dwellers I see that Jahveh was the desert in
all its naked heat moving up to consume the baalim of settled
communities, who had exchanged the rigorous asceticism

imposed on them by the desert life, for a sensual indulgence which the previous starving had only enhanced. Job, of course, was an Arab, and his present day progeny stand in the same relation to Allah as he stood in relation to Jahveh, so passionately asserting his own individuality against that engulphing one-ness. How far 'the eternal illusion' as I might call it, took hold of your own mind, I can guess, and yet in all your overt acts you are only harnessing its power to serve some temporal and even momentary ends, in which you do not altogether believe, at least not with the spirit of worship which you feel towards the power it was your business to subjugate and canalise. That's the whole moral problem: one not very different in kind from that confronting Paul on his road to Damascus. As I read your book, and it is a riddle, that is the conflict which subsists at least implicitly under the material action of the book. Or is it some bent in my own mind which forces me to consider you sub specie aeternitatis?

You don't simplify any of these problems by your method of treatment. Probably you are too restive under the limitations of the medium in which you work. You are one of those writers who are not content that writing should be a continuous action, and try to precipitate their thought and feeling into an instantaneous act. Having a sudden completeness of vision, complete in all its detail, you try to represent it, immediately, as you see it, and tend to pack a clause too full of meaning. One cannot present an object to the vision simply by enumerating, with however nice a precision, all its qualities. You have an amazing richness and variety of expression, and there are descriptive passages — I recall one about Rumm — which have a vivid beauty of mass and colour and light; but I think the descriptive portion of the book slows down the narrative. You only needed as much topography as might show the way the country influenced your action: so much in short as the action could carry with it. A narrative should always tend toward the dramatic, and the book is definitely a narrative, with its superb dramatic moments such as the death of Farraj or the last ride of Tallal to death: splendid moments. Description necessarily recedes from the dramatic aim. You do them so well, too; but take an occasional fault in diction, 'dolerite' or 'striated': think of the brake which words such as those put on the speed with which one must apprehend the object presented. They are only casual blemishes, but they illustrate what I mean about descriptive passages slowing down the dramatic action. The minuteness with which you describe a scene in all its variety while seeking to compress it even by the use of technical terms leads at times to a kind of obscurity. It is very brilliant, but the brilliance has now and again a restless dazzle which prevents clear vision.

I never care to talk much about style. It is like faith, if you consider it too closely you lose sight of its object. I have a fairly clear idea of what I want to do in writing, and probably that makes me less likely to be a sound critic of others. Your prose has almost a solid and tangible quality: it is musical, 'numerous' in the right sense of the word; and parallel to the architectonics of its method is the accumulation of material. After I had read it through with little intermission, I found the impression it left a little confused, as though it reflected the complexities of style: and whatever those complexities may be their effect should be simple. When I re-read passages, even lengthy passages, I do not feel the same difficulty. It seems clear and definite but if I continue long enough the other impression recurs. The constant repetition or succession of vivid detail tends to blur the whole.

After seeing you the other day I was inclined to tear this letter up. You looked in good fettle and gay-complexioned: as though you were finally done with Arabia, and the responsibilities fastened on you. The book is the record of quite another mind, thwarted and unhappy on the whole. Most of us who served during the war in any capacity were left with a feeling of vexation, caused I think by the fact that the will had passed beyond its object, and in the completeness with which it had attained its end found only emptiness less. It took some time for the waters to subside and clear. To me your book, however I may criticize it is a great action: it has the reality of action. I do not mean of the action it describes, but the action it is. I found it profoundly interesting because it leaves me asking myself and you and life so many questions. I am inclined to think you destroyed the first draft of it, because you had been too frank and angry in it, and what we have is your first compromise with fate.

136

Perhaps I should have torn this up, after all. It is too long if
that be its only fault, which is unlikely

Yours always
Frederic Manning

Answered by D.G. 416

Printed heading

20.vi.30   Garland's Hotel, Suffolk Street, Pall Mall, sw1

Dear Shaw:

Distrusting my own ability as a packer, I took The
Seven Pillars to Davies' office yesterday, and asked them to
forward it for me. Then a series of chance meetings kept me out
all day, and until late last night, so this note will not reach you
until the book is in your hands, returned, apparently, without
ceremony. I do not know whether you like ceremony, but I rank
it, myself, among the fine arts. Unfortunately I am perhaps too
much of a philosopher to be an artist, and too much of an artist to
be a philosopher. This has impressed itself on me since I have
been revising Scenes & Portraits.

It was very kind of you to let me keep the book so long. I
wanted to look at it again. You should be more content with it;
but that to an artist is a counsel of perfection. It is really something more than a great book, it is a great experience.

I should like you to return to it from another angle. No: I am
by no means suggesting that you should re-write it, but I wish
you would write: 'A Dog-fight in Downing-Street':[1] a spare,
ascetic, brief and impartial account of the conflict of interests
there, with indifferent portraits of the combatants: too indifferent
even to be cynical. For that, one needs a mind trained to a very
sinewy baseness and a style almost mathematical in the precision
of its terms.

I am longing to read Mint.

137

If chance bring you to Town you might load the dice a little in my favour. I shall be here anyway until next Saturday.

Yours always
Frederic Manning

¹ *T.E.L. had written of his struggle for the post-war settlement of the Arab countries:* For two years there was a dog fight up and down the dirty passages of Downing St., and then all came out right (D.G. 416).

Printed heading

13.viii.30   Garlands Hotel, Suffolk Street, Pall Mall, sw1

Dear Shaw:

I should be enormously interested to see Mint in type-script, however greatly I may deplore the decision not to print. Off-hand, and at a venture, as I have no notion of what it is like, I should say that you do not probably appreciate the fallacy on which these decisions are usually grounded. When you wrote it you thought it was right; and now you yourself have changed, after having given it a more or less immutable form. It is not likely that you should be more right now than you were then: though the disparity between then and now may seem to show up a few imperfections, perhaps only necessary and inherent in the material: material being a term which covers yourself as well as circumstances represented and interpreted by you.

I do not really wish to influence you in the matter, even if it were possible, as I take it that your own purposes must be clearer to you than they are to anyone else: only the most characteristic of our actions are usually those we regret, either because our memory of them becomes confused with later phases, which makes them seem imperfect, or from a kind of vanity which refusing to admit the change in our own minds finds them insufficient. They were not worthy of us, we say, without modesty.

On the other hand, I do not see why you should spend £120 to print 12 copies for a gift to your friends: it is quite enough for you to give them the book. And printed or typed I do want to see it, whatever you may think of its form or style. Style and form do not interest me to the extent they once did; I am more absorbed in the difficult language of facts, which by its own nature achieves both spontaneously.

The Apologia Dei[1] moves very slowly: it is difficult, and there are too many inevitable distractions, teeth among others, to disturb me. Still I think it is going the right way.

I am wondering whether I shall see you again, before October when I go abroad. I shall be here for a fortnight

always yours
Frederic Manning

I think you will like 'God' when you read it.

---

[1] *An additional piece for the new edition of his* Scenes and Portraits (1930), *dedicated* To T. E. Shaw.

Printed heading

29.x.30   Garlands Hotel, Suffolk Street, Pall Mall, sw1

Dear Shaw:

The child I am fathering on you has gone to the printer, and I shall say no more about it than that it was conceived in sorrow, and brought forth in pain: you will have to decide for yourself whether you will own to the brat or not.

I shall be going off to Rome in about three weeks' time, and if there should be a chance of seeing you in the interval I should welcome it. I shall be at The Node, Codicote, Hitchin for the next ten days, but can come up.

You have broken faith with me about Mint, or so I think; but perhaps you were only waiting until I had disentangled myself from the divine mysteries of creation.

In the interval I see that you have been in Turkestan; as you have apparently the power of being in two places at once: El Harith, the busy one, who makes mischief among the slippers of the faithful, outside the mosque!

Well, God bless you in all your ways Mint or no Mint. As I put the last words to the Apologia Dei yesterday they fired a royal salute in the Park. Wasn't it nice of them?

Yours always
Frederic Manning

* *Printed heading*

12.i.31   The Node, Codicote, Hitchin, Herts.

Dear Shaw:

I assume, as I have not heard from you, that you are disappointed in the Apologia Dei. Also I retract all previous protests, and admit I am a stylist and more of a stylist, probably, in the Apologia than anywhere else. You are, I think, a friend of E. M. Forster and I wish if you ever write to him you would tell him how pleased I am that he liked the book. I have always liked his work, his point of view, and way of writing. He has individuality. I should like to tell him so myself, but it would seem immodest. A man called Bonamy Dobrée gave me a very good notice in The Spectator.

So much for mine own affairs. I heard, on Lady Astor's authority, that you are leading a quiet, useful and respectable life; but for the recent ramp against the prayer-book (caps) she would have said sober, righteous, and godly. There's some conflicting evidence which holds you responsible for troubles in Afghanistan, Turkestan, and an attempt to overthrow Stalin: as tho' you were el-Harith himself. If you have these talents I wish your conscience would drive you out of the Air Force to head a revolution here at home. There is much to be done with a broom. I wonder if you thought that for you parts of the Apologia were intended to have an esoteric significance?

140

Ross has asked me to pay him a visit, and I should love it. Oriel under Shadwell made Oxford seem a mother to me. But to-morrow I go to The Bull Hotel, Bourne, to write my romance: the runes work only in eclipse.

Yours always
Frederic Manning

About a dinner with Sir Francis H. Humphrys, High Commissioner and Commander-in-Chief of Iraq

Printed heading

28.viii.31   Suvretta House, St. Moritz

Dear Shaw:

You should have written to me long ago. I break the silence myself, only because you may be amused to hear that I have met Feisal. Sir Francis Humphreys, whose name I always mis-spell, asked me to dine with him. Two Italian royalties, the Duke and Duchess of Pistoia were present, so there was a certain amount of ceremony: but only enough to be decorative.

But Theodoli, the Italian representative on the League of Nations, and head of the Mandates Commission, interrupted my conversation with the King. He was engaged in some manoeuvre concerning oil & roads. I was amused to watch Feisal playing them, while Cäetani held me with talk. I think the King was annoyed with them, but smooth; only I thought some ironical spirit gleamed in his eye.

I did not mention your name, but later Giafar Pasha[1] spoke of you to me. He said you were the bravest man he knew; but I said very little even to him. I thought that perhaps you don't care to be talked about.

I think you might like Humphrys. He knew from the Privates you knew me.

I go back to London tomorrow: I hope better than when I came here. I shall be at 26, Gilbert St. Brook St. w.1 until Sep 5th so if fortune brings you to Town let us see each other.

yours always
Frederic Manning

¹ *Ja'far Pasha al Askari was then the Iraqi Minister for Foreign Affairs and Defence.*

21.xii.31   The Bull Hotel, Bourne, Lincs.

Dear Shaw:

In sending you my best wishes for Xmas and the New Year, I have an uncomfortable feeling that I should have written to you earlier: but I have not been really well for the whole of the past year, and one of the most marked features of my infirmity is the lassitude which succeeds to an attack. However, I am mending, and if I can keep it in check through the winter it may become quiescent again. It has prevented me from doing any satisfactory work, and Peter is very disappointed; but really even if it were finished, at present Peter is only fit to publish the banns of his approaching marriage. I want to get it done, for the purely selfish reason that I wish to be delivered of it.

Are you interested at all in contemporary Russia? And have you read a book called Without Cherry Blossom, by a younger member of the Bolshevik party called inappropriately Romanov? I can't understand why people want to read Shaw's account of Russia, when they can read Romanov. They would probably object that Romanov's picture is an imaginative fiction, and that Shaw's account would be a record of historical fact; but even if their distinction were right the historical fact is always an isolated, and particular fact, and to enumerate a whole series of such facts does not make the sum of them less partial, or more complete. Romanov's people are all lunatics living in a nightmare; but he has an extraordinary insight into the psychology of women; and his characters are really living people. Emil Ludwig and his wife were glorifying Shaw to me at St. Moritz and I said that Shaw's dramatic genius was entirely in the representation of action, that he had never succeeded in creating a real character, that his people were merely types, though the way they were related to each other gave them a semblance of life. They resisted the argument without much heart, and eventually agreed. Wassermann, an Austrian novelist, supported my point of view. They suggested Candida (who is no different from his other women). I should have suggested the heroine of Captain Brassbound's Conversion but only, I think, because I saw Ellen Terry in the part.

Should you be in London during the next fortnight I shall be at The Alexandra Hotel, Hyde Park Corner, s.w.1; and it would be very cheering to see you

Yours always
Frederic Manning

Answered by an unpublished letter, of January 2nd, 1932, in which T.E.L. referred to the conversation about G. B. Shaw: As for persons in his plays, I regret to report (with a horrid grinning pleasure too) that I appear in an indecently thin disguise as Private Meek in his new play 'Too True to be Good'

Printed heading

4.i.32   The Alexandra Hotel, Hyde Park Corner, sw1

Dear T.E.S.
        I shall be up here now until the 21st, as on that day my Mother and sister go to Rome, en route to Sydney, where Lang, the Premier of N.S.W. has given us an example of what

143

the application of Shavian theories in political practice may produce. It is a comedy for everybody not involved in it. Shaw I have only met once at Lammer;[1] but my feelings for him have always been of mingled affection and aversion.

As a small boy, (or not very small, about 16), I was taken by Max to see You Never Can Tell; and Max, and G. Street, and A. B. Walkley discussed in one of the intervals how it might be possible to rescue Shaw from undeserved neglect. The result was a series of articles in The Saturday, Blackwood's, and The Times which were, I think, effective. Earlier, Candida had been a success; but after the production of You Never Can Tell to which I refer, Shavianism became a cult. Perhaps my affection is due to the fact that I assisted at the birth of a vogue. My aversion is from the sophist, who is too Protean to be refuted cursorily: one would have to follow him step by step, for he colours his premises with assumptions which he draws from them again as the irresistible conclusions of logical argument. Life's too short. He's a case for the Nietzschian psychologist, a case of perversion: and with what N. called his 'thoroughly mob-like & Jewish resentment' no one could be less Nietzschian than he is. But I often wonder what spiritual tragedy warped him into that direction.

The name Meek, I take to be an example of the Shavian irony, & Lucifer, son of the morning! (Lucifer I believe was a king in Babylon, whose fall Isaiah contemplates with so much satisfaction as to allow of commiseration as well.) Your 'grinning pleasure' is at the after-thoughts his portrait leaves you to indulge. Can you play upon this pipe? No, he would never pluck the heart out of any mystery.

I am very much better. I shall go back to Bourne when I leave this place, and try to gratify Peter's insatiable appetite for another book. You must have quite good fun at your testing. Do you test hulls for speed? White whose life I compiled conducted some of the early researches into the problems of form. He was delighted when a Viking ship was dug up, having the exact proportions of a destroyer he had designed. If I remember rightly the coble is one of the forms offering least resistance.

yours always
Frederic Manning

144

Ludwig's Napoleon, I haven't read, but I do not care for Ludwig's other books which have come my way. He gave me July 1914. Personally, he amused me especially his moments of comic and bewildered honesty.

¹ *The house of Apsley Cherry-Garrard, G. B. Shaw's neighbour.*

26.iii.34 Buckingham, Wentworth St., Point Piper, Sydney

Dear Shaw:
[*Three sentences omitted*] Yesterday evening was wonderful, quite incredible in fact: the east all delicate mauves and greys, and in the west clouds, like burnished copper, barring a sky, that passed through imperceptible shades of difference from palest yellow, and greens, through turquoise, to an absolute peacock blue. I watched it until the moon had changed everything to lead and quicksilver ... [*Three sentences omitted*]

Yours always
Frederic Manning

17.vii.34   Gleneden, Burleigh Road, Bourne, Lincs.

Dear T.E.
Where are you? Did you call at the Bull while I was in Australia? If you did, it was rather odd, because I used to have a feeling that some day you would turn up there. I now lodge with a married daughter of the late landlord: humble, but comfortable circumstances. If you come to visit me here, I shall give you my Heal bed, and dispose myself on the sofa, as most nights I have to sleep sitting up. Coming home I read Too True to be Good and Liddel Hart's book, and I saw that the author of 'I, Claudius' thanked you in his preface. I didn't care for 'I,

Claudius', but imagine the author is better than his book. I can't believe that Claudius felt, or thought, or wrote like that.

Do let me hear how, and where, you are. I have just come from Cambridge, where I met a nice man called Pickthorn, who belongs to Corpus Christi.

Yours always
Frederic Manning

26.vii.34   Gleneden, Burleigh Road, Bourne, Lincs.

Dear T.E.

Graves's book is really a crime in itself. I have always considered Caesar, Augustus, and Tiberius as quite respectable examples of 'l'homme moyen sensuel'.

The Agrippinas were pretty dreadful. How prompt their satirist was to sentimentalize over any of the royal house who died young 'breves et infaustos populi Romani amores'.

I shall be very glad to see you. Some impulse prompts me to send you the enclosed. A curious face: I imagine a bandit, beaten into subjection by this coster-monger age. You may recognize a friend, who knows?

The News-Chronicle had a disgraceful leader on the Dolfuss murder; almost excusing it. And next to the leader a portrait of Sir Stafford Cripps. The Austrian question is more likely than anything else to cause a war.

Probably you will feel leaving the service: but we all have to re-create ourselves from year to year. Clouds Hill, Moreton, Dorset! What a perfect address!

Yours always
F.M.

Gleneden, Burghley Street, Bourne, Lincs.

Dear T.E.

I fear that your bicycle was ready for delivery sooner than you anticipated, and that the chance of seeing you has diminished. When I read of some flying boats going to Iceland, I wondered if you were of the party. I saw they were going to Oban, and I thought they might pass by Craignish Castle where my friend Colonel Gascoigne lives. He's a man you would like, though he is over eighty. He went with Sir Charles Wilson in the last desperate endeavour to save Gordon, and I believe they got into Khartoum half an hour after Gordon had been killed. Getting away with some wounded, a traitor on board wrecked the steamer, and Gascoigne got the wounded away over the desert. I was told he should have had the V.C. for it but he was not even mentioned in despatches, as he was not there 'officially'. He had been in the Blues, but at the time I think had been taken on in some capacity by the Camel Corps. He was in S. Africa; and as soon as the last war broke out went to France and drove an ambulance, until, to get him home, they put him in charge of a reserve battalion. I gave him Liddell Hart's exposure of you, which he liked. Of course Hart should have mentioned the Parthians. Gascoigne gives all his time to sailing at Craignish.

I was wondering also, whether the increase in the Air Force might help you to an extension of service. You might like it; but on the whole I should imagine that you were finished with that experience and have got what you needed from it

Yours always
Frederic Manning

I have forgotten your regimental no. Is it 388171?

21.xii.34   Gleneden, Burghley Street, Bourne, Lincs.

Dear T.E.

I wish you a merry Xmas and a happy New Year. Personally I enjoy more an unpremeditated feast, and perhaps feel most at home with a bun on Good Friday.

While I was in Town I read here and there in your Odyssey, and need I say I liked it, as I expect to like everything you write. Of course I may boggle at a word occasionally, as at 'twittering' of the handmaidens' feet, when hanging: tho' 'twitching' might not sound so well.

Also I looked at Claudius the God and decided that it was much better than I, Claudius: the manner more fit for the time and characters. But it does not fit in with my conception of Claudius himself. To be rather demodé in my illustration, I think an admirable representation of unconscious self-portraiture is A Prince of Court Painters.[1] Graves' method suits Messalina better than it suits Livia, and I noticed a slightly repentant after-thought on Livia's account.

I shall be in London, at 26, Gilbert St. Brook St. for five or six days from the 3rd Jan, having been told to use the house as mine, while the owners are away: not that I shall use it as mine, but I shall be alone there

Yours always
Frederic Manning

[1] *Walter Pater's study of Watteau in* Imaginary Portraits.

EZRA POUND
1885-

Typed except for last paragraph   *Embossed heading*

20.iv.20   5, Holland Place Chambers, Kensington, w

My Dear Hadji ben Abt el Bakshish, Prince de Mecque, Two-Sworded Samurai, Old Bird, Young Bird, Magister (?) Artium, etc. et quid tibi licet, libet, decet, lubet, etc.:
    Thou hast in thee an exceeding hot, intemperate, swift and precipitate manner of judging thy fellowe men, and in the present case mightest have weighed against six or eight pages of BLAST the dozen or more volumes and thousand or more scattered pages of my other labours and opusculi.

The Dial is an aged and staid publication which I hope, rather rashly, to ginger up to something approaching the frenetic wildenesse of The Athenaeum. They are much more afraid of me than you are.

Also I don't care a saffron ... whether you use your own name or not; only if you don't you will be under the shameful and ignominious necessity of writing something which will interest the editor.

Can you 'write'? Of course, having vortex'd a large section of Arabia you are fed up with vortices; but why reprove me, who have merely created a market for one or two artists and got a half dozen good books into print despite John Murray, Sir G. Macmillan e questa puttazaia?

When you say you want to write for money, what do you mean 'money'? Lord McCauley's rates, or the fees I pick up by force of necessity to pay my rent. The latter can't be called 'money', but if you want to sweat in an abysmally paid profession I think I can supply you with two London editors who wouldn't insist on your using your cinema sign.

In sending copy to America, let me caution you to use an incognito as well as a pseudonym. Thayer is, I think, quite decent (He is the Dial), but I trust an American publication

149

about as far as I wd. trust a British government; my bright compatriots are quite capable of printing an article by Mr Smith, and then printing a leetle note at the end of the number saying 'The article by Mr Smith is really written by the distinguished Shiek tamer and Tiger-baiter etc. ... who for reasons of modesty has concealed himself 'neath the ridiculous name of Smith-Yapper'.

If you want to write about Arabia, I cd. simply write to N.Y. that I was getting copy from the one man who knows, or you cd. get a written promise from Thayer not to reveal your identity. I shd. prefer not to be instrumental in publishing anything likely to incite either Moslems or Xtns. to further massacres etc. The songs of the desert might be safer. My notes on Elizabethan Classicists are considered 'too technical' for the Dial readers.

I have just taken on the job and can't, I am afraid, give you much indication of what they do want, save that I am asked to provide 'em with Mrs Meynell, Lowes Dickenson, Lytton Strachey, Yeats, Eliot, myself in homeopathic (very) doses, etc.

Hope to see you in August, if not before — — Shall be back here in Aug. — Suppose you'll have spent your quarter's allowance & retired to Oxford by then

Yours
Ezra Pound
20/4/20

Typed except for last lines   Embossed heading

[? August 1920]   5, Holland Place Chambers,
                                        Kensington, w

Dear T.E.L.

Being neither a Christian, nor an Oxonian, nor even an Englishman, the idea that people 'ought not to exist on one earth' merely because they differ one from the other is strange to me.

Doubtless you have <u>very</u> bad taste; not that I mind the romantic, or even the academic and idylic, if they can be found free of mental paralysis.

Still ... I have already sent over to N.Y. one hundred delicious pages of Manning, which I hope will in due course be printed; and Conrad has said he will probably send on something some day or other, but has too many unfilled promises hanging over him to make any more; and two stories (or somethings) by D. H. Lawrence have been accepted ... through no particular fault of my own save that I asked Aldington to ask D.H.L. to send 'em in.

And Aldington gets steadily worse <u>because</u> he writes in the Times every week ... what <u>can</u> be expected !!!!!!!!!!!!!!!!!!!!!!!!! !!!!!!!!!!!!!!! (these by request, as you'd feel lonely if I didn't use 'em, in order that the skripture shd. be fillfulled.)

I suppose I'd even print Hodgson (whom I like personally very much) ... chief danger wd. be going to sleep between here and the pillar box if I had a mss. of his in my hand ... tel est le pouvoir ...

Is Yeats any worse than the last volume of Conrad's? [*Added in ink*] & as for idyllic & romantic — thought they were W.B.Y's particular line — howsomever.!

Yours sincerely
Ezra Pound

SIEGFRIED SASSOON
1886-

16.viii.[23]   54 T.S.

Pshaw dear! (If anyone else has made that 'joke' already, I apologize.) What you say about Recreations[1] is good reading for me. When people — whose opinion I value — are

151

encouraging about my career, I feel a giant. You would be doing me a good turn if you were to loan me a copy of the Seven Pillars. The fact that you interest me profoundly would make even a dull book by you interesting. The little I read of the Seven P's made me think 'here is a book I could spend many a quiet day with.' So send it, there's a good mystery motorist.

Now; I hope I haven't done anything which will annoy you. (vide H.G.W.'s card). The fact is, I met him[2] this evening at a club where he was dining alone, & he told me he was going to Swanage for 3 weeks, — tomorrow. And had just returned from Berlin, Paris, Prague, etc. Had it in my mind that I must write to thank you for your nice letter & ask for your book, so how could I have helped wanting you to have a nice talk with H.G.W. So I told him that you were within easy distance of Swanage, & he said, 'give him my address, & let him do whatever he feels like'. Personally, I think HG. is a tremendously important fact in our 'thought-riddled age', & I like the idea of your mind clashing with his.

But I have a curious feeling about 'bringing people together'. It gives me a creative feeling! (You did meet HG. once, didn't you?) Have I done the wrong thing? As a matter of fact, knowing you is a source of secret satisfaction to me. (apart from your standing the test of closer acquaintance). I would like to go about boasting that I know you! But I don't, really. I despise myself for wanting to do it ... And, good gracious, you make me write like a school-girl who would 'love to have your autograph — '

SS

---

[1] Recreations (1923); *copy inscribed* T.E.L., S.S., 2.8.1923.
[2] *H. G. Wells.*

152

Upon reading the draft version of Seven Pillars. *On December-
ber 16th,* 1923, *T.E.L. sent the letter to Edward Garnett,
with comments* (D.G. 233)

26.xi[23]   54 T.S.

<u>Frost & Fog, 5 p.m., etc.</u>

   Dear ?
              After fumbling a couple of Choral Preludes by
Bach (to invoke sincerity) I take my pen in 'and ... 'that book.
Is any of it worth while?' you ask.
   The marker stands at Ch. 86. so I am 8 chapters ahead of my
schedule. And my existence since the Turners went to Italy
(on Oct. 1.) has become increasingly nocturnal & self-indulgent
& cerebral. Sitting here sipping china tea & pipe-puffing by a
bright fire while Westminster bells punctuate eternity, (they
haven't heard about Einstein yet,) I have savoured your Hejaz
hardships. Have, in fact, enjoyed all the fun without so much as a
grain of sand in my cup or the least touch of dysentery! How I
adore your under emphasis of the literary achievement, you
'amateur writer'! ... But —
   R. Hodgson was here one night lately, & we were discussing
the bardic existence. He said, The writer who is any good must
doubt & doubt the quality of his work, & go on doubting. —
   When R. Graves told me (bicycling along a road in August
1921) that you'd written a hell of a good book, I was incredulous.
(In those days you were, to me, a myth which I mistrusted.)
Granted that you'd <u>had</u> the amazing experiences, I couldn't
believe that you'd been so fortunate as to get them down on paper.
Well, as far as I'm concerned, you <u>have</u>.
   I was intending (regardless of HG.W.) to wait until I'd got to
the end; then try & see the thing as a whole, (at present I am a
fly on the map of Arabia); & then run rapidly through it once
more, on the striding red she-camel of my critical faculty, in an
effort to estimate the style, & to test by a second reading the
effectiveness of your occasional (& most appropriate) swank-

descriptions. But you have precipitated my gratitude for the boon-companionship of the book.

I am a lazy, desultory reader, & I abhor small type — How can you explain my 25 days-sustained interest, except by admitting that the Seven Pillars is damned interesting? Am I a good judge of a prose style? Perhaps not. But I know all about con-densation, & I haven't felt the least sign of diffuseness — . On the contrary, I've felt as if you'd been given the last bale of paper in the world to write your book on, & you'd never forgotten that you mustn't put in an unneccessary word, (in Ch. LXXVI. you say 'we mustered together', — I could spare that 'together').[1] Yet there is a leisurely ease about it all, — the camel moving smoothly & well within her-self — I haven't ridden one but I use the metaphor horsily). Damn you, how long do you expect me to go on reassuring you about your bloody masterpiece? It is a GREAT BOOK, blast you. Are you satisfied?, you tank-vestigating ere-mite —

[*A paragraph omitted*]

I was reminded of you at Roberts's exhibition[2] — (I pur-chased a drawing of some ghastly ghouls 'in a Café', for £30, out of sheer admiration for the efficiency of the workmanship.)

'The Owl'[3] has arrived this afternoon. Sorry you left out the old woman who sent you the 'pleasant little Baluch carpet'.

I have been niggling away nocturnally at my verses, & have finished a few more 'Recreations' & a 'Meditation on Modern Militarism', which I sent to Brailsford's Labour weekly. I haven't dared to think about it since, but will send it to you when it appears. It may be all right, but I am not yet sure, till I see it in print.

Reading Dill's 'Roman Society in the last Century of the Western Empire' I came across the following. 'Alliteration & assonance, pompous periphrasis taking the place of simple expression of ordinary fact, antithesis without real contrast, outrageous hyperbole, & the most excruciating puns, — all these vices were cultivated by Sidonius, with a melancholy waste of effect' — It made me wonder whether we live in a similar age, & whether some of my recent efforts aren't rather Sidonian!

But I am beginning to focus life a little, & to realise how few things are worth while, & how very worth while the few things are. Does that sound priggish. Do come out of your tank soon.*

SS

* I think I understand why you are in it. (I felt like going down a coal-mine myself four years ago.)

Dec. 6th

Well; it is finished. I take off all the hats I ever wore — to you, & it. You alone know how it could have been bettered. I can only say that you make your effects without fail. (& always, it seems, by your great literary gift of not using an unneccessary word.) As autobiography it succeeds greatly. As an exciting, incredible, narrative it has never let me down. As a historical document I've no capacity to judge that.

The whole achievement, lived & written, is (can't find an adjective which doesn't sound gaseous & silly.) And I'm going to read it again, — every word of it. I've never read a satisfactory epic before, — (not being a classical scholar I can't talk about Homer.)

I feel ashamed of all these superlatives, but you've worn me down & swept me away, & I know the achievement to be great. At the end I turn back to that infinitely touching story of Farraj & his friend which made me cry when I read it ... Having suffered from 'Chauvels',[4] I must add that I am extra-thankful that a great war-narrative (& criticism) has been written by one who is the same sort of human being as

SS.

Be happy; you really have pulled it off.

And, O, how I love to think of the thwarted publishers, & the frustrated reviewers! Hooray, hooray, hooray, good book.

[1] *In the draft,* Then we mustered together in a whispering group on the clammy grass. *In the final text,* Then mustered, whispering, on the clammy grass. (*The chapter number has been changed to that in the final text.*)

[2] *Many drawings by William Roberts were reproduced in* Seven Pillars.

³ The Winter Owl, *edited by Robert Graves, included an abridgement of three chapters of* Seven Pillars.

⁴ *Mr Sassoon does not remember what he meant by this word, which to the Editor looks like a combination of 'Chauvinists' and (Paul) 'Claudel'.*

Upon reading The Mint

13.xi.30 (1.30 a.m.)   23 Campden Hill Square, w8

(That bit about Queen Alexandra is wonderful).

Dear T.E.
          Your letter is undated, but it must be a full month since I received your typescript, which I have just finished — I could say a lot about it, but I fear my comments would be mostly irrelevant — (i.e. speculations about my own mental & physical condition as stirred up by your fearless revelations, — which amount almost to an acute physical experience for the reader). There is no doubt that you have got it down on paper all right. But then you are an extraordinary writer — I doubt whether you could increase the impact of its flesh & blood realities by re-writing it. Of course some of it is, superficially, a bit of a shock to one's squeamish mind. But if the characters talk & act like that, how can it be omitted? The problem of writing about life becomes more & more difficult. The only solution seems to be — writing for oneself (& someone, like E.M.F. — if there are any more people like E.M.F. — & he is in the same dilemma, I suppose).
     So I arrive, inevitably, at myself! Your book is a drama of mind versus body, — isn't it? You resent 'coddling' your body, & resent the d — d apparatus altogether. Often, while reading, I stopped & queried 'Can one achieve internal harmony', or mental 'perfect fitness', or whatever it is — in defiance of physical comfort? Here am I, with my gas-fire & my arm-chair, — trying to be austere & aloof, — aware that adventures of the

156

mind (or spirit) are desirable, — detesting dinner-jacketdom & social security, — yet, in an hour or two, I shall be boiling a kettle & filling the rubber hot-water bottle which enables me to get to sleep! What is one to do with the body, when it is so obviously 44 years old, & vitality has to be artfully conserved? I can't write books or react to the richness of experience when I am tired or have a sore-throat & a headache. The soup of the Reform Club steams for me, & I travel by train because driving my Packard fatigues me — I complain that my mental life is distracted because I have to write about 30 negative letters a week to editors, strangers, people I have 'lost sight of for years', & old friends who desire to view me oftener. Meanwhile, you, apparently, have escaped all this. Lucky you!

Your book has also reminded me rudely of the gross brutality of 'unprotected' human existence. How can one go on writing lyrics in the presence of physical facts, (such as age, ache, penury, & imprisonment, plus the faces one sees in the streets of London, & the conventions & false refinements of people one, if possible, avoids knowing) — ? Also there are the innumerable runners-away from reality, — cinema-doped, music-doped, wine & spirit doped humanity — human beings doping themselves into believing that their activities are 'important' — — 'I'm terribly busy — 3 committee meetings this afternoon' — 'must get my new novel finished,' 'Have to write a long article,' etc. And O, those booming clubmen at the Reform, with their glasses of port, & their awful acquiescence! Well, well ... I am writing to a real man, anyhow — And Blunden has written a good introduction to the new edition of Owen's poems — (published next Feb. I hope). So let us march on, & remember that we have not always been found (physically) wanting.

Yours ever.
SS.

14.xii.[33]   Fitz House

Dear T.E.
       Can you be there next Monday — at Christchurch Priory — 12.30? The ceremony should interest you, & your presence would be much valued by the 2 protagonists. There won't be more than 20 people there, at the most. It will give me an opportunity also of introducing you to Geoffry Keynes, — a man you ought to know.

                                  Yours ever.
                                      SS.

P.S. No top hat.

Written when T.E.L. was semi-permanently stationed at Bridlington, for work on R.A.F. speed-boats

Printed heading

8.xii.34   Heytesbury House, Wiltshire

Dear TE.
[Four paragraphs omitted]
I lunched at Bridlington on Nov 13th. 1931. when I was motoring R. Hodgson to Scarborough & back. I never saw a seaside place look so forlorn! The girl who served us with poached eggs said 'It's enough to make a girl go wrong.'

                                  Yours ever.
                                      SS.

In reply to D.G. *547, upon his* Vigils

Printed heading

19.xii.34   Heytesbury House, Wiltshire

Dear T.E.
        Every window of has been lit up by your letter, &
Hester is sending up mental rockets regardless of expense. I am
sending you a chart of dates. I can't deduce much from them
myself, except that the 1929-30 ones were about all the verse
I did in that period of exhaustion by ordeal; whereas the 1932
batch were selected from a fair amount of intensive scribbling.
After Sept. 1933 complete silence set in; but thank heaven I
have done quite a lot of verses in the past 2 months — several of
which seem likely to be added to 'Vigils' when I reprint it —
perhaps next autumn — It remains to be seen & judged, whether
what I do now will have more vigour & movement in it. It
'ought to have' — I was — in 1932-33 — losing hopefulness about
my personal future. A sort of dreary feeling was setting in. Now
I live in a sort of 'permanent future', & feel rather like an
embodiment of the four seasons, — winter nothing to worry about
& spring a certainty.
        I hope my increasing terseness won't develop into a mannerism.
        I penned a jocose sonnet a month ago which will amuse you.
        'When urged to write — in prose — another volume, I feel my
powers unequal to the labour (though pleased to think of possible
emoluments it might bring to self & Messrs. Faber and Faber).
"Reconstruct" says one adviser, "life in perspective." "Mix
yourself with fiction", remarks another. Wanting to be wiser, I
ruminate their views without conviction.
        'I must condense immense experience, transmute huge masses
of acquired material, and put my life on paper while I lead it. I, a
fly, it seems, must now commence to codify the solid and aerial
world that I buzz in. Fellow flies will read it.'
                                        Yours ever.
                                        A. Fly

In pencil

> In a world simply seething with troubles,
> The three most unburstable bubbles
> Are Hitler & Goering & Goebbels.
>
> In a world of suspicions & squabbles,
> The one plan that works, though it wobbles,
> Is Goering & Hitler & Gobbles —
>
> In a world that bleats, bellows, & babbles,
> Hitler & Goering & Gabbles,
> Bamboozle obedient rabbles —
>
> I dont think I've ever been wearier
> Of any three names than of those:
> And I'd give any number of roubles
> If somebody'd lead to Siberia —
> Each one with a ring through his nose —
> Hitler & Goering & Goobles.

G. B. SHAW
1856-1950

Cf. *Blanche Patch*, Thirty Years with GBS (1951), *chapter v*

In reply to D.G. 161

25.viii.22   Priors Field, Godalming
(until the 30th)

    My dear Lawrence (to drop ceremony)
        First, <u>business</u>, as if I were your solicitor.
There is not the <u>smallest</u> doubt (within human limits) that any
publisher would jump at your book on Arabia; and there is no

Oct. 6th

Well; it is finished. I take off all the hats I ever wore — to you, & it. You alone know how it could have been bettered. I can only say that you make your effects without fail. (& always, it seems, by your great gift ~~literary~~ of not using an unnecessary word.) As autobiography it succeeds greatly. As an exciting, incredible, narrative it has never let me down. As a historical document ∴ I've no capacity to judge that.

The whole achievement, lived & written, is (can't find an adjective which doesn't sound gaseous & silly.) and I'm going to read it again. — every word of it. I've never read a satisfactory epic before, —(not being a classical scholar I can't talk about Homer.)

I feel ashamed of all these superlatives, but you've worn me down & swept me away, & I know the achievement to be great. At the end I turn back to that infinitely touching story of Farraj & his friend which made me cry when I read it . . . ✗ Having suffered from 'Chauvels', I must add that I am ~~~~ extra-thankful that a great war-narrative (& criticism) has been written by one who is the same sort of human being as ♪.

Be happy; you will have pulled it off.

And, O, how I love to think of the thwarted publishers & the frustrated reviewers! Hurray, hurray, hurray, ~~good luck~~!

[*actual size*] see page 155

The Royal Hotel. Knysna C.P. South Africa.
18th February 1932

I have surpassed all my previous exploits as a motorist by driving our hired car at full throttle over a ditch and hedge surmounted by 5 lines of barbed wire, through a bunker three feet deep (a sunken path), and to a standstill in rough country with one strand of barbed wire wrapped round the propeller shaft. Neither the car nor its driver were disabled; but you must make Lady Astor shew you the letter I am sending her by this mail detailing the consequences to poor Charlotte. She is lying up here quietly for repairs, all other arrangements being cancelled; and our earliest possible appearance at Southampton will be the 11th April. The 2nd May is more probable. The catastrophe has escaped the press so far: be discreet.

G.B.S.

[actual size] see page 181

doubt at all that the book, having forced itself from you, will be published with whatever imperfections its mortal lot may involve, whether you like it or not. May I suggest it to Constables? You may as well make up your mind to it.

Second, as man to man. It will be pure waste of your time for me to read your book before you send it to press; but it would not waste mine, as I shall read it sooner or later. But at this moment I am at the Fabian Summer School at the above address. On the thirtieth I go to Glastonbury for a few days and then on to Yorkshire for a week at the Labour Research Department's Summer School. I am travelling light, and have hardly a chance of reading the paper, much less 300,000 words. So will you let the reading stand over (if you would still like me to do it) until after the 10th. Sept. or thereabouts, when I shall pick up my wife (now in Ireland) and return to our country address, Ayot St Lawrence, Welwyn, Herts?

You need not stand on any ceremony with us. You are a privileged soul, and can deal with both of us as with old friends.

I should have answered this before, but have been interrupted again and again: you see I have had to cook the date[1]

ever

G. Bernard Shaw

Answered by D.G. 165

[1] *He had altered 23rd to 25th.*

Typed   *Printed heading*

1.xii.22   10, Adelphi Terrace, wc2

My dear Lawrence

Patience, patience: do not again shoot your willing camel through the head.

The truth is, I havnt read it yet. I have sampled it; but I must read it all through. My wife seized it first, and ploughed through from Alpha to Omega. It took months and months and months; but it carried her through. But the time it took warned me that I must dispose of certain other reading jobs, in respect of which I was tied to time, before tackling it. Then came the election, which obliged me to throw over everything and take the road tubthumping.

However, I know enough about it now to feel rather puzzled as to what is to be done with it. That, you may say, is your business; but the Life Force will take it out of your hands. Obviously there are things in it that you cannot publish. Yet many of them are things that WONT die. It would cost too much to engrave the whole book on plates of gold, and bury it somewhere for somebody to dig up and start in business as a prophet.

One step is clear enough. The trustees of the British Museum have lots of sealed writings to be opened in a hundred years. From time to time as the centuries lapse these sealed packets are opened, and are generally found to be destitute of the smallest interest. Sir John Soane left relays of such revelations: one of them was opened only the other day; but the veil of the temple was not rent in twain. I myself made Kate Perugini deposit some letters of her father (Charles Dickens) which she was on the point of burning. The suppressed chapters of Oscar Wilde's De Profundis are there, waiting a resurrection fifty years hence; and I, having read them, can testify that there is nothing in them to make the smallest fuss about.

You say you have four or five copies of your magnissimum opus. At least a couple should be sealed and deposited in Bloomsbury and in New York. If a third were buried in Rome or Paris or Washington, the book would be fairly fireproof.

Think this over: I am sure to suggest it when I am through with the reading, which is now under weigh. Destruction of the work is out of the question: if I thought you capable of that I should take the book to London, burn down my house here, and tell you that the book had perished in the flames. It is one of the Cheops pyramids of literature and history.

I estimate the number of words as at least 460,000. No matter: I read the Bible in my youth straight through from Genesis to the

Epistles; and I daresay I shall survive your seven pillars. But an abridgment will have to be made for general circulation. There is a need for the main history of a campaign for working purposes. For real human interest and for military usefulness a detailed record of the failures and wreckages and spiritual vicissitudes knocks all the historical outlines into a cocked hat; but it doesnt matter whether such a record is that of Caesar's campaigns in Gaul or Lawrence's in Arabia. At the other end of the scale comes the Encyclopedia article, from which you want no vicissitudes, but dates and particulars of the frontiers that were shifted as a result. Between the two comes the Thucydidean history, giving the bones of the affair but making them live.

However, I am anticipating. Besides, you know all this as well as I do.

I am curious as to how you will come out of it — out of the reading I mean. Take the case of Gordon, for example. He was a most infernal scoundrel according to any workable standard of human morality. Yet that does not account for him at all. Have you ever considered the question as affecting yourself? You are evidently a very dangerous man: most men who are any good are: there is no power for good that is not also a power for evil. I am an Irishman; and on the only occasion when I spent a day or two in Turkey I was struck by the fact that the Turk is everything that the Englishman imagines himself to be, and happily isnt. I might easily have devoted myself to a vendetta against the English Turk pro the Irish Arabian, like Erskine Childers: there was as good a case for it as yours against the Turk. But I didnt: on the contrary, I saw that in that sign the Turk would triumph. You have a conscience which would have prevented you from acting as Gordon did in China; so there will be a deep difference; but I wonder what, after reading the book through, I will decide to do with you if ever I become one of the lords of the east. As I shant, perhaps I shall put you into a play, if my playwriting days are not over.

ever

G.B.S.

P.S. In case it would amuse you to see us at any time we are fairly accessible in the country as well as in London (where we spend little of our week now). Hatfield is only half an hour from Kings Cross; and I have a small car in which I could run you seven miles to our house here if you give me notice. Our London days are mostly Thursday and Friday.

Answered by D.G. 184

In reply to D.G. 184: The book is being abridged. Edward Garnett, a critic, has cut it to 150,000 words, and I'm going to see if a publisher will pay for these miserable orts

Typed   *Printed heading*

17.xii.22   10, Adelphi Terrace, wc2

My dear Lawrence
      I knew of course all along that publication was inevitable in the simple operation of the laws of nature; but until you told me about the Garnett abridgment and so forth I held my tongue. A day or two after, I happened to have to discuss a question as to the price of some new editions of my books with Constables; so I blew in there on that business, and, being in conference with William Meredith and Otto Kyllmann, the two senior partners, I led the conversation eastward to Yemen and Colonel Lawrence. It turned out then that Meredith had met you and knew about the Sybilline copies. I naturally said 'Why in thunder didnt you secure it? it's the greatest book in the world'. He said he should have very much liked to, but felt that he could not push for it without indelicacy, and could only hope that it would come his way.
    I then expatiated on the qualities of the work, and said that it really ought to be published in the good old eighteenth century style in twelve volumes or so to begin with, the abridgment coming afterwards. This is not at all so impossible as it would have

been ten years ago; for people are buying very expensive books now on an unprecedented scale, whilst my early novels in Constable's shilling series have gone out of print for the moment because cheap books do not sell.

Anyhow, they became intensely interested; and yesterday I received a letter from Kyllmann. He had been rather afraid of cutting in across any arrangement that you might have made, and had accordingly seen Garnett and ascertained that he was acting in his private capacity and not as reader to an already selected publisher. Kyllmann's letter runs 'I wonder if you would be so very kind as to tell Colonel Lawrence that we should be very pleased and honoured to be entrusted with the publication of his book ... If I knew what he wanted as to terms etc. we would do our best to meet his wishes.' The rest is covered by what I have already said.

This abolishes all approaches and preliminaries in case you would care to deal with Constables: you have nothing to do but come straight to business with them. If not, there is no harm done. But I don't think you can do better unless you would prefer a brace of thoroughgoing modern ruffians who would begin with exploiting the serial rights in the American and English papers with headlines and pictures and all the rest of it. Of course Kyllmann could sell the serial rights for you as well as any other agent; but you could do that without his interference if you wanted to. The point is that with the modern ruffians all the rest of the business would be of a piece with this; and you never could get them to see more than six months ahead. With Constables you would be more comfortable and most respectable. You would find it possible to talk easily and understandably to Meredith and Kyllmann after your manner. They know your value, whereas the ruffians would know only your sales, being incapable of history. If you decide against Beaverbrookdom, you will have only a few firms to choose from; and Constables will be one of them. So now you can consider it at your ease.

Your letter is more impressive than explicit. If I knew nothing else about you I should conclude that you were a depressed mechanic oiling up fuselages for profanely abusive pilots, and sleeping six in a bed with a hundred other such castaways. As it is, I can only pity the staff. Nelson, slightly cracked after his whack on the head in the battle of the Nile, coming home and insisting on being placed at the tiller of a canal barge, and on being treated as nobody in particular, would have embarrassed the Navy far less. A callow and terrified Marbot, placed in command of a sardonic Napoleon after Austerlitz and Jena, would have felt much as your superior officers must in command of Lawrence the great, the mysterious, save in whom there is no majesty and no might. The thing is ridiculous. Why in the name of all that is sane did you not get £20,000 from parliament? It was yours for anybody else's asking, if you rule out your own; and you should have demanded it as your obvious right.

You talk about leave as if it were a difficulty. Ask for three months leave and they will exclaim, with a sob of relief, 'For God's sake, take six, take twelve, take a lifetime, take anything rather than keep up this maddening masquerade that makes us all ridiculous.' I sympathize with them. If you must be a Cincinnatus, go and farm. If you must be a Garibaldi, live at Caprera instead of putting poor Aldershot out of countenance.

Of course you know your own affairs worst; so I tell you how they strike me. Also, damn it, I want to know the other half of what you have told me. One can guess nothing about a man capable of anything, like Habbakuk. Are you a flying officer or a bloke in a military office? It would be so like you to be charading as an office boy.

distractedly,
G. Bernard Shaw

Answered by D.G. 187

28.xii.22   Ayot St Lawrence, Welwyn, Herts.

My dear Lawrence

The cat being now let out of the bag, presumably by Jonathan Cape with your approval, I cannot wait to finish the book before giving you my opinion, and giving it strong. IT MUST BE PUBLISHED IN ITS ENTIRETY, UNABRIDGED. Later on an abridgment can be considered, though it may take the shape of a new book, like Wells's Short History of the World following his Outline of History. But anyhow you must not for a moment entertain the notion of publishing an abridgment first, as no publisher would touch the whole work afterwards; and I repeat THE WHOLE WORK MUST BE PUBLISHED. If Cape is not prepared to undertake that, he is not your man, whatever your engagements to him may be. If he has advanced you any money give it back to him, (borrowing it from me if necessary), unless he has undertaken to proceed in the grand manner with a library edition in several volumes. But you can borrow all you want from your banker on the security of the book without being obliged to anybody; only as the banker would charge you interest, and the security is as good for me as for him, it would be cheaper to borrow from me.

My wife, who believes fanatically in your genius, wants to know why you withdrew your preface to Doughty's book. She read the preface at her club, and immediately ordered a copy. It came without the preface and with different pictures. She sent it back indignantly, and now demands an explanation. Do you feel disposed to indulge her with it?

I did not see the nine guinea new Doughty, because when I was on the point of the outrageous extravagance of ordering it I was told that it was very carelessly proofread. You must be very careful about the Seven Pillars on this point, because corrections are now very expensive; and you may easily get let in for them unless you know your way about as an author.

The truth is, I am anxious lest you should have committed

yourself already. I had ten years on the managing committee of the Society of Authors, and learnt that there is no bottom to the folly and business incompetence of authors or to the unscrupulousness of publishers, who, being in a gambling business where one live book has to pay for ten duds, cannot afford to lose a single opportunity.

You must not mind my shoving into your affairs like this. How else can I be of any service? Still, it's rather maddening; and I feel quite as apologetic about it as I ought.

ever,
G. Bernard Shaw

[*Added in ink*]
P S Did you get my last quite recent letter?
Answered by D.G. 191

Sent with a cutting from the Daily News *of the same date, announcing that T.E.L. had enlisted in the R.A.F.*

Typed   Printed heading

4.i.23   10, Adelphi Terrace, London, wc2

My dear Lawrence,
        Like all heroes, and, I must add, all idiots, you greatly exaggerate your power of moulding the universe to your personal convictions. You have just had a crushing demonstration of the utter impossibility of hiding or disguising the monster you have created. It is useless to protest that Lawrence is not your real name. That will not save you. You may be registered as Higg the son of Snell or Brian de Bois Guilbert or anything else; and if you had only stuck to it or else kept quiet, you might be Higg or Brian still. But you masqueraded as Lawrence and didn't keep quiet; and now Lawrence you will be to the end of your days, and thereafter to the end of what we call modern history. Lawrence may be as great a nuisance to you sometimes as G.B.S. is to me,

or as Frankenstein found the man he had manufactured; but you created him, and must now put up with him as best you can.

As to the book, bear two things in mind about me. First, I am an old and hardened professional; and you are still apparently a palpitating amateur in literature, wondering whether your first MS is good enough to be published, and whether you have a style or not. Second, I am entitled to a reasonable construction; and when I say, as I do, that the work must be published unabridged I do not mean that it shall be published with the passages which would force certain people either to take an action against you or throw up their jobs. The publisher would take jolly good care of that if you were careless about it. But these passages are few, and can be omitted or paraphrased without injury or misrepresentation.

As to style, what have you to do with such dilettanti rubbish, any more than I have? You have something to say; and you say it as accurately and vividly as you can; and when you have done that you do not go fooling with your statement with the notion that if you do it over again five or six times you will do it five or six times better. You get it set up, and correct its inevitable slips in proof. Then you get a revise and go over your corrections to see that they fit in properly and that you have not dropped one stitch in mending another. Then you pass for press; and there you are. The result has a certain melody and a certain mannerism which is your style, of which you are no more aware than you are of the taste of the water that is always in your mouth. You can, however, try an experiment. Copy out half a page of the work of some other man, and you will find your hand so rebelling against his particular melody and mannerism that you will have to look at the original after every second or third word to prevent yourself from getting off his track on to your own. The moment you are conscious of style in your own work, you are quoting or imitating or tomfooling in some way or other. So much for style.

Now as to the book just as it is. You will no more be able to get rid of it, or to play about with it, than with Lawrence. It is another Frankenstein monster; and you must make up your mind to do the will of Allah, in whose hand you were only a pen. You say that to publish anything now might look as though you were using the

R.A.F. as an advertizing stunt. Considering that you have already used the whole Arab race and the New Testament and the entire armies of all the countries engaged in the war to advertize yourself (since you take that view of it), I do not see why you should have a sudden fit of the bashfulness of the lady in reduced circumstances who cried laces in the street but hoped nobody heard her. A long deceased friend of mine, a parson, once told a drunken carpenter that there was once a carpenter who gave his life to save him. 'If so', replied the reprobate, 'you may bet that he did it to get his name up'. You must get used to the limelight. I am naturally a pitiably nervous, timid man, born with a whole plume of white feathers; but nowadays this only gives a zest to the fun of swanking at every opportunity. If you read my works with the attention they deserve they would have cured you of this misplaced modesty, which is precisely what makes Rahab assure you that she is only a clergyman's daughter. The officer who saw a first rate advertisement for the R.A.F. in your enlistment shewed a much finer appreciation of the situation. And the people have their rights too, in this matter. They want you to appear always in glory, crying, 'This is I, Lawrence, Prince of Mecca!' To live under a cloud is to defame God.

Moral: do your duty by the book; and arrange for its publication at once. It will not bounce out in five minutes, you know. You have the whole publishing world at your feet, as keen as Constables, who have perhaps more capital than Cape. Subject to that limitation you can choose where you will.

The other day Sidney Webb stayed with me for a week end. I put the book into his hand and said 'Read a couple of pages of that and tell me how it strikes you.' As he reads a book almost as fast as he can turn the pages, he took quite a large dose in ten minutes, and then said 'George Borrow — not that I ever read George Borrow'. 'What do you mean by that?' said I. 'He describes every blade of grass he walked over' said Webb. I told Mrs Webb that there was something in it about her nephew Meinerzthagen. She did not find it; but she gave me his South African dossier. Funny, your meeting at the Colonial Office!

Forgive the length of this; but as you never think unless you are down with dysentery in an Arab tent with the thermometer

100° above the temperature of hell, I must do your thinking for you. That is the worst of the Army: a soldier stops thinking instinctively. If he didn't he wouldn't be a soldier. With which gibe, farewell until your next folly.

Ever
G.B.S.

[*Added in ink*]
P S We are going down to Bournemouth for a week on Satur-day. Chine Hotel, Boscombe, Bournemouth.

Upon receipt of a package of his own letters to T.E.L., returned by Mr Cope Hand who had found it lying in Lombard Street

Postcard   Printed heading

9.i.23   The Chine Hotel, Boscombe

Just read the enclosed. I suppose you were practising bomb dropping and aiming at the Bank of England, though why you should use such a flimsy projectile as my letter beats me.

I have told Mr. Hand that the letters are your property and that he must hold them until you reclaim them.

Charlotte (my wife) says 'Something extraordinary always happens with that man' (you).

I shall be here until the end of the week.

G.B.S.

About his attempt to secure a pension for T.E.L.; he had given the Prime Minister, Stanley Baldwin, a copy of Robert Graves's publication, The Winter Owl, *which contained an abridgement of Chapters LXV–LXVII of* Seven Pillars

Typed   Printed heading

11.i.24   10, Adelphi Terrace, London, wc2

My dear Luruns,
            I have again seen the P.M., and presented him with a copy of The Owl as a sample of the famous history. I gave him a vivid description of your success in making the army ridiculous, and told him that Hogarth was mistaken in supposing that you had any objection to a pension (he said that he had got nothing out of Hogarth) and that I had your own authority at first hand for saying that you would accept one. I explained that your objection was to being forced to exploit your campaign for a living as a literary man, and not to having it recognized by the country in the proper way.

He said his difficulty was that as the Civil List, a scanty and eleemosynary affair, was no use, there was no way of getting a pension except by a vote of the House, which at the present juncture was impossible. I said, What about a military pension? He had not thought of that, and made a note. And there we left it. He was as pleasant as possible, and is taking The Owl down to Chequers to read about the Turkish Delight gelatine, the slaughterousness of which ought to clinch the matter.

Charlotte banged twelve and sixpence on The Owl under the impression that it contained something new by you, and was at first indignant at being put off with a chapter of the book of books. But when the P.M. wrote next day, she recognized the finger of Providence.

I should add that I suggested that the military authorities, in the matter of the pension, should take the attitude of the corporal to whom you reported for elementary instruction, and close all ranks to you in future except that of Field Marshal.

Ever
G.B.S.

T. E. Lawrence, Esq.
 Clouds Hill,
  Moreton,
   Dorset

Answered by D.G. 239

Typed   *Printed heading*

7.iii.27   10, Adelphi Terrace, wc2

My dear Luruns
   Your letter to Herself has just arrived. The press-cutting is a journalist's notion of paraphrasing my preface to the Leicester Gallery exhibition catalogue.[1] When the paraphrase has been paraphrased ten removes or so you will do well to avoid reading the papers. I have just sent in the review of Revolt in the Desert to The Spectator. That, too, will be paraphrased; so look out. They have an ingenious way of stopping short half way in my sentence about the Government leaving you to make money out of the book, so as to create an impression that you are rolling in royalties like Churchill and his war book.

On Thursday last Barrie not only announced a dinner for married bachelors at Adelphi, but actually brought himself up to the scratch and gave it. Baldwin, Grey, Sir Donald Maclean and myself hobnobbed with him for nearly three hours. Baldwin said you had sent him a set of the Pillars. He was much pleased and said he must write to you; so I gave him your address with a copy of the catalogue. I mean to have that pension yet, not that I am under any delusions as to All Souls in Oxford or No Souls in Blenheim, but because, being old, I know that you will be hurled

173

out of your monastery before you can say Jack Robinson seven times; and then where will you be? Besides, you ought to have money to chuck about. Heaven means that patronage should be dispensed by the like of you. Finally, when you are too old at forty we shall have to support you if the State doesnt; and though we should like that, you wouldnt.

In the Spectator review I have hailed Kennington as the Perfect Screever. A screever (in case you dont know) is a pavement artist. The portraits produced that effect irresistibly in the gallery. I like Kennington. He is a real character without being at all characteristic, which is an effect new to me. You and I are worse than characters: we are character-actors.

My book,[2] which has stretched to 180,000 words already, is within a chapter of its end. It would have been finished but for my being defendant in a lawsuit which is set down for the 14th. My counsel and solicitors having reduced themselves to mere insanity over it I have had to lay out the case for them in critical communications which are Institutes rather than letters.

G.B.S.

[1] *Eric Kennington's portraits of Arabs.*
[2] The Intelligent Woman's Guide to Socialism and Capitalism (1928).

In pencil

12.iv.28   Oakwood Park Hotel, Conway, N. Wales

Dear Auranshaw

Get your mind clear about The Mint — if it is possible to get your mind clear about anything that smells of ink. It is a document of record, made at a cost of experience and with a literary power that makes it rare and valuable as a record. There is not the slightest reason why it should not be shewn to anyone

174

interested in the manners and customs of soldiers, or the psychology of military professionalism, or the history of initiation rituals, or the taming of animals, or half a dozen other departments of history and science. The slightest reticence or self-consciousness about it would be misplaced and unpardonable.

As it cannot be published as a work of literary art (except possibly by Werner Laurie in a three guinea subscription edition as pure bawdry) the only thing to be considered is how and where to place it on record and to secure it from destruction. Such records are always in great danger in private hands; and even in public hands they are not inviolable. For instance Francis Place, the Radical tailor who ran the Reform Bill of 1832, had a craze for record. He left diaries, press cuttings, patterns of materials, all sorts of things. They are now in the British Museum. In the diaries he kept a record of the language of himself and his playfellows when he was a poor boy in the streets of Whitechapel. But his pious son carefully cut out all the bad language (inheriting a talent for the scissors) before handing the stuff to the Museum. That has happened over and over again.

Within my recollection the Museum keepers destroyed a set of designs (XV century Italian, I think) as too obscene even to be hidden away. I have never heard of their destroying an authentic written document; but there is sufficient possibility of this to make it desirable that copies should be planted in various quarters.

The question is, what quarters? The United Service Institution. The War Office. The British Psychological Society. The College of Physicians. The British Museum, Bodleian, Cambridge, Dublin, Edinburgh &c. The ci-devant Imperial Libraries of the Continent, especially Russia and the Republics which have an interest in facing what the military retinues of Kings (the soldier is a survival of the King's footman) are like. Of course the librarians would have to be sounded first; but they all have top-shelf books which are not accessible to the general reader and can be procured by specialists or serious students only; and they all like to have special possessions of one sort or another.

This being done, everything will be done that you could possibly have contemplated when you did the job; and you may dismiss it from your mind and go on to something else.

Question remains, where are the copies to come from, as all this will cost money? Solution: sell the manuscript to Foyle for the cost of producing and distributing an edition of 20 copies.

Alternative solution (ignoring Werner Laurie): publish a Bowdlerized edition through Cape. This is not impossible: a lady can stow things in the corners of her heart as lyrically as elsewhere. I once travelled in a train full of reserve men called up for South Africa. They were drunk; and when they were not yelling competitive descriptions of what they were going to do to old Kroojer (homosexual variations on the traditional torture of Edward II at Berkeley Castle) they were weeping on my neck about their wives from whom they had parted at Waterloo, leaving them resourceless. I got in at Guildford and got out at Haslemere; but as far as language is concerned all your Depot experience was compressed into that half hour. Yet I published an account of the journey in (I think) The Clarion which fell short of your report in little except precise philological information. And when, as in the case of the slang for soldier, paraphrase is impossible, one can always fall back on a dash.

Still, though you are wobbling between your conceptions of the thing as a verbatim report for the archives and a work of art, I think you had better discard the latter unless you are prepared to rewrite a good deal of it with humor enough to make it bearable and decency enough to make it presentable, and then let Cape publish it on condition that he supplies also the 20 unexpurgated copies for the archives.

So much for business — except, by the way, that if you have contracted to give Cape the refusal of your next book (which does not tie you as to a private report) you must fulfil your obligation in the customary sense without attaching any unforeseen and unusual conditions. But of course Cape need not demur to any of your extravagances. He will be perfectly ready to give you an agreement to publish on Garnett's advice, or even against it, knowing that the proof sheets must pass through his hands, and that if they contain an obscene, seditious, or blasphemous 'libel' you cannot compel him to publish or the printer to print, agreement or no agreement. So that is all poppycock. You cannot play with the law as you played with the Medina-Damascus railway.

Now as to the Mint itself. There are only two passages which I should scrap. In the military policeman's story of the dead child in the harlot's bed, you forget, in the middle of it, that you are supposed to be reporting it as it was told, and allow yourself to drop into a descriptive passage of pure Literary Lawrence that smells of the lamp almost as rankly as the policeman smelt of the brothel. It is a purple patch; but it doesn't fit, and should come out.[1]

Then, as to Queen Alexandra and Miss Knollys and Dighton Probyn. The picture is Hogarthian, granted. The street boy that is in us all grins at it. But — seeing that parliament cannot give these people a bottle a year of the elixir of life — is it their fault that they grow old? If Probyn could not keep his palsied head steady or his mouth shut: if Alexandra could not prevent her rings from slipping about on her wasted fingers or produce a natural head of hair for you instead of a simulacrum, need you savagely exult in her infirmities, and, as Lessing puts it, not only chop her head off but hold it up to shew that there were no brains left in it? You allege absolutely nothing but simple senility. Probyn at worst was no worse than a Struldbrug. To Alexandra's complexion your mother will come at last, as you yourself will come to Probyn's, if you both live long enough. Would you like George to read your description of his mother? Would you like to read a similar description of your mother, however powerfully artistic? Be human, you young ruffian; and either scrap that description or recast it nobly and generously.[2] Take it out of the parson if you must take it out of somebody.

I wrote very unceremoniously to Robert Graves under the impression that he was Charles, whom I treat sans façons. His book is not all to the good. Biographers, like portrait painters and sculptors, put something of themselves into their subjects and sitters when there is anything of themselves to put in. In Robert's hands your exploits become a series of puerile atrocities; and Auda becomes an incorrigible old swindler. There is only too much to be said for both views: indeed they ought to be put forward by the devil's advocate when your time comes; but that was not Robert's job; and it should be done thoroughly and intentionally or not at all. You will probably do it yourself some day.

177

I have many other things to say to you; but this letter is long enough, and had better be confined to the practical aspects of The Mint.

ever
G.B.S.

Answered by D.G. 357

¹ *Retained but altered in the final text* (*Part III, Chapter* 12). *In the manuscript version:* A neighbouring court, whose precipitous tenement-walls pushed the night-cap dome of London's smoke-mist almost sky-far away, so that its arc refulgence hardly modified the blackness of the pit.

² *Retained in the final text, with minor alterations which heightened the effect* (*Part III, Chapter* 9). *T.E.L. commented to E. M. Forster:* Shaw says it's the meanness of a guttersnipe laughing at old age. I was so sorry and sad at the poor old queen (D.G. 364).

In reply to D.G. 363: I have thought of a night-watchman job, in some City Bank or block of offices. The only qualification for these is Service experience

Typed

21.x.28   Ayot St Lawrence, Welwyn, Herts.

My dear Luruns
          The first qualification for a night watchman in Threadneedle St is a capacity for taking the Bank of England seriously, and an unfeigned respect, mounting to religious awe, for the Governor.
          I know a man who was medical officer to the Great Western Railway. In the days when I was still investigating labor questions I asked him were the effects of night work as bad as it suited agitators to allege. He said <u>no</u>, PROVIDED ALWAYS the night worker behaved all day as if it were night and all night as if

178

it were day. This involved finding some place to sleep where there was no more noise than there is at night. Meals precisely as if ante-meridian were post-meridian. On these conditions the nocturnal habit of mind and body was soon acquired; and the owlman was as healthy as the cock that crowed in the morn.

But it is to be remembered that he was speaking of railway workers, whose night work is open air work, and who therefore get more ultra-violet rays (darkness is brief in summer) than the booking office clerks and their like. A night watchman in a bank would not enjoy this advantage. He should therefore provide himself with one of the new Sunray electric lamps, and bask in it between his rounds.

An imaginative novice with a literary turn, not afraid of solitude or ghosts, and extremely fed up with his fellowcreatures, may picture himself as a night watchman sitting in lonely groves of bags of gold, pouring forth in perfect peace page after page of immortal verse or prose, or inventing hitherto unconceived algebraic methods, or even simply reading novels. What the reality is like I do not know; but I guess it as a very exacting sort of sentry-go, on which an armed man paces through a nightmare of rooms and dungeons, every one of which he must visit once every hour, and every one furnished with a clock (you may have seen one at the National Gallery) which will betray him if he does not do something to it at hourly intervals, and may even shew its sense of his neglect by ringing the tocsin and turning out the guard. I should say that after a week of it you would return to the Colonial Office like a lamb, unless indeed half a dozen safes had been rifled whilst you were writing to Charlotte, and you had been arrested for connivance.

When a Sultan becomes a beggar for seven years to cure himself of paranoia (or whatever is the scientific name for swelled head) the cure will be so complete at the end of five years that he will find it necessary, in order to avoid going mad in the opposite direction, to throw off his rags and become, if not a Sultan again, at least a Cadi or a fig merchant.

Having taken that trick I await your next lead.

ever
G.B.S.

About a proposal that Jean Forbes-Robertson should take the leading part in Edward Garnett's play, The Trial of Jeanne d'Arc; *also about an accident to a flying-boat* (cf. D.G. 433)

Printed heading

8.ii.31   4, Whitehall Court, London, sw1

Dear Luruns

What I make of Garnett's letter is that Jean F.-R. does not want to play his Joan and has cast me for the part of Mr. Jorkins. Fortunately I am able to play it quite effectively.

I have sent an epistolary wink to Jean, and written to Garnett to explain that she would most certainly give mortal offence to the highly influential Council of the Royal Academy of Dramatic Art if she anticipated her first appearance as Joan as fixed for the great Gala performance which is to rescue the R.A.D.A. from the desperate financial straits into which it has been plunged by the falling-in of its lease and the demolition and rebuilding of its premises on a scale far beyond its means. If I were to die tomorrow it would make no difference: she dare not disappoint the rest, who include her father, Ainley, Du Maurier, Barry Jackson &c &c. So Edward must wait. I cannot alter the situation.

As to the crash, you seem to be in the position of the sentinel in Macbeth who, having seen Birnam Wood start to walk, could say only 'I should report that which I say I saw, but know not how to do it'. You are a simple aircraftsman: nothing but an eyewitness's police report can be extorted from you. However, as you will probably insist on conducting the enquiry, and as you will want to save your ambitious commander from being sacrificed, the future, to my vision, is on the knees of the gods. Pray heaven they sack you!

Charlotte is in bed with a swamping cold in London.

G.B.S.

Postcard

18.ii.32   The Royal Hotel, Knysna C.P. South Africa

I have surpassed all my previous exploits as a motorist by driving our hired car at full throttle over a ditch and hedge surmounted by 5 lines of barbed wire, through a bunker three feet deep (a sunken path), and to a standstill in rough country with one strand of barbed wire still holding. Neither the car nor its driver were disabled; but you must make Lady Astor shew you the letter I am sending her by this mail detailing the consequences to poor Charlotte. She is lying up here quietly for repairs, all other arrangements being cancelled; and our earliest possible appearance at Southampton will be the 11th April. The 2nd. May is more probable. The catastrophe has escaped the press so far: be discreet.

G.B.S.

ELLIOTT SPRINGS
1896-1959

In reply to D.G. 452. *About his diary of the Royal Flying Corps,* War Birds, *which he had published anonymously and later attributed to his dead comrade, Lt. MacGrider*

Typed   Printed heading

25.ix.31   Lancaster, S.C.

Dear Shaw:—
Your letter arrived and not only did me a great honor, but was tremendously flattering. It will go a long way toward removing the sting that was left by the critics when the book was published. Practically no one over here liked it. My

181

father denounced me bitterly, Mac's family wanted to sue me for defaming his character, the old women cried out for my scalp, the professional writers shouted 'fake', and I shut up and to this day have never told anyone how much of it came from where. I gave the money from it to his two children and told his sisters to sue and be damned. A few busybodies checked up and found out that Mac was killed during his second week at the front and exposed me as the knave.

You suggest that I annote a copy of it for history's sake to show how it grew. That is just what I don't want to do. If it lives, I want it to live as Mac's diary, not as my novel. The controversy will be forgotten in a few years and then perhaps the book may be revived and read by a new generation on its own merits. My hope is that it will be a monument to Mac's memory. He has no other.

I did everything I could to keep my name away from it, though I did not realize at first that it was going to be difficult or important. Everyone discouraged me with it and I had practically given up any idea of publishing it when a magazine suddenly began to exploit it.

However, to show you how much I appreciate the honor you have paid me by your letter, I am sending you by Nelson Doubleday my original manuscript in pencil which will show you exactly how it developed on paper. You will note that I wrote fast. I think I did the whole thing in four days. I used parts of Mac's diary, my own diary, my combat reports, my letters home, and some official reports.

I hope some day you will come to America and visit me. Then I can show you all the original sources of the book. They are too bulky to send to you and would mean nothing without a personal explanation.

I think you are right about the writings under my own name. When I am forced to supply a fictional background for the material I had to leave out of WAR BIRDS, I lose my grip on the reader. Did you read CONTACT and LEAVE ME WITH A SMILE? If not, I will be glad to send you copies of them.

My father died in April and since then I have become president and managing director of some fifteen corporations which include everything from a bank to a railroad. Needless to say, I shall never have a chance to write again. I have had to give up flying as I have no understudy or sergeant-majors, and I suppose I will have to give up drinking next. It is only recently that I have been able to drink again. I had to quit after I was shot down in June of 1918 and wasn't able to take it up seriously again until I had an artificial stomach put in about four years ago.

I love England. Someday I hope to go back for a visit. I was there in 1921 but saw nothing but ghosts and only stayed a month.

I am sorry too that I didn't know more of the rank-and-file, but you must bear in mind that they would have none of us. We tried to cultivate them but they didn't care for officers or cadets, and even less for Americans. But practically all of our fellow officers in the R.F.C. were ex-Tommies. Perhaps I do not make that clear in my writings. Social life in the R.F.C. was always a little difficult for us to understand. The American army is a very democratic affair, and we sometimes made it very difficult for the British commandants.

Again I thank you for your letter. If you feel that you are writing to a legendary person, I have the idea that I am writing to a mythical one. I think I should not post this letter but burn it up the chimney as I used to do with my messages to Santa Claus.

With all good wishes,

Yours,
Elliott Springs

338171 A/C T. E. Shaw,
R.A.F. Mountbatten,
Plymouth, England

LORD STAMFORDHAM
1849-1931
(*Then Private Secretary to King George V*)

About the report published by Robert Graves, Lawrence and
the Arabs *(November* 1927*), of an audience with the
King, at which T.E.L. refused to accept decorations. In reply
to a letter which T.E.L. wrote on the same day as one to a young
friend:* Graves sent me an advance copy of his book. I'm
relieved to find only two things in it which hurt — one, the
story ... The other is my interview with the King. Neither
his account (called mine) nor Lord Stamfordham's very
exactly fits my memory. I had never a notion of fighting the
British in arms: nor was I quite as priggish as Graves
makes out (D.G. 329)

Royal crest and printed heading

New Years Day 1928   Windsor Castle
as from Buckingham Palace

Dear Shaw
         I conclude this is now the name which you wish to
bear —

It was good of you to write to me and your letter of the 7th
Decr. last was read by the King.

When Graves asked permission to allude in his book:
'Lawrence & the Arabs' to the incident of your asking permission
to decline the decoration conferred upon you by the King I
necessarily had to refer the matter to His Majesty: and transmitted to Graves what H.M. told me remained in his memory of
the interview with you on that occasion. From what you say the
impressions left on H M's mind does not coincide with those
remaining on yours. But the King says, It is now nearly 10 years
since the conversation took place: and while it is obviously
impossible to remember the actual words used I believe that
Lawrence said that he had given his word to Feisal and as
apparently the British Govt. was not going to keep its word &

184

that probably he (Lawrence) might be fighting with the Arabs against British troops, be taken prisoner or killed 'he did not wish to be found wearing the ribbons of British decorations' —

I must tell Robert Cecil the story you quote when I next see him — !

Graves' book is full of interest especially to us who have not read the 'Seven Pillars of Wisdom'.

My old friend Mrs. Hooper of Massachussets in her last letter says: 'I have lately read every word of Lawrence's precious book & I am more & more grateful to you' — So you at all events made one elderly lady happy on the other side of the Atlantic — !

I am very glad to gather from the concluding paragraphs of your letter that you purpose coming <u>home</u>: and can more than realise what that word must mean to you.

I may also add that the King was pleased to know of your intention —

If you will permit me to say so: you ought not to be '338171 A C Shaw' residing in Room 2 E R S. R A F. Depot at Karachi: but your proper place is at home amongst men & women of intellect and culture like yourself.

I think you told me you rather liked, or did not mind, scrubbing barrack floors & tables! but is this not misuse of those physical powers to which your splendid services with the Arabs testify?! Nor can I imagine that your great endowments of mind derive any benefit from such occupation? unless it is a case of 'lying fallow' after excessive cropping!

Please let me know when you arrive in London as I hope to see you under whatever name you may elect to adopt. With best wishes for 1928.

Yours very truly
Stamfordham

17.i.28   Buckingham Palace

Dear Shaw,

  In continuation of my letter of New Year's Day, I write to let you know that since then I have found the record made on 31st October, 1918, by Colonel Wigram of your conversation with the King the previous day, and the following is an extract from the record:

  During the course of the conversation, Colonel Lawrence said that he had pledged his word to Feisal, and that now the British Government were about to let down the Arabs over the Sykes Picot Agreement. He was an Emir among the Arabs and intended to stick to them through thick and thin and, if necessary, fight against the French for the recovery of Syria.

  Colonel Lawrence said that he did not know that he had been gazetted or what the etiquette was in such matters, but he hoped that the King would forgive any want of courtesy on his part in not taking these decorations.

You will note from this that His Majesty, speaking from memory, thought you had expressed a determination to fight if necessary against British troops, whereas you only mentioned French troops. I am anxious however that this slight discrepancy should be cleared up at once.

Yours very truly,
Stamfordham

33817 A.C. Shaw
 Room 2 E.R.S.
  R.A.F. Depot
   Drigh Road, Karachi.

Though it was at a private audience that T.E.L. refused the insignia of C.B. and D.S.O., rumours circulated that he had done so in the midst of a ceremonial investiture (cf. articles by Churchill and Isham in T. E. Lawrence by his Friends, 1937

and 1954, *and the revised text of the former in* Great Con-
temporaries). *The gesture therefore both attracted more
attention and caused more harm to T.E.L.'s reputation than
he can have anticipated. But it produced the results he desired.
In Sir Winston's words, it* opened my eyes to the passions
which were seething in Arab bosoms. I called for reports
and pondered them. I talked to the Prime Minister about
it — *and, two years later, effected a settlement (utilizing
T.E.L.'s advice) which rectified Arab grievances so far as lay
within Britain's power*

AIR VICE-MARSHAL SIR OLIVER SWANN
1878-1948
(Then *Air Member for Personnel, Air Ministry*)

*Instructions for T.E.L.'s first enlistment in the R.A.F. These
arrangements were made by order of Air Chief Marshal Sir
Hugh Trenchard, whose letter of July 20th, 1922, foreshadows
them and establishes that he had Ministerial approval*

16.viii.[22]   Air Min.

Dear Lawrence
        I have made the following arrangements:—
You will present yourself at the RAF Recruiting Depot
Henrietta St Covent Garden at about 10.30 A.M. on August
21st.
    You will say you wish to see Mr Dexter from whom you have
had a letter. Flight Lieut. Dexter will interview you and will fill
up the necessary forms — you should tell him the particulars we
have arranged upon. (Not the whole truth, nor your real name).
He will advise you as to the age to give & what trade to enter in

— (Dexter knows you are being specially entered & will help, but does not know all the facts, which do not concern him).

You will then be medically examined at Henrietta St. Do not mention any disability. If you are passed all will be well. If you are failed, F/L Dexter will arrange matters.

You will have to produce two references as to character & previous employment during the last two years. I leave you to procure these. They will not be investigated but it is necessary for you to have them in order that someone may not say that your papers are not correct.

You will be sent to Uxbridge with a draft of recruits — At Uxbridge you will be attested & medically inspected —You will have to declare that what you have stated on the attestation form is correct & you will have to swear allegiance to the Crown. You will be given a slight educational exam if you are entering as an aircraft-hand.

I trust that there will be no difficulty after leaving Henrietta St. No one will know about you after leaving Henrietta St: but if any difficulty arises, as a last resort, ask that Mr Dexter of Recruiting Depot be communicated with by telephone.

Please let me know if the above does not suit you. Otherwise I shall do nothing until I hear from you —

Yours sincerely
O. Swann

A reference to your case will be kept by CAS & myself & Deputy Director of Personnel

Your name is John Hume Ross.

An account of how medical objections were overruled is given in T.E.L.'s letter of thanks, D.G. 166, above which is printed a note written by Swann some fifteen years later: I never met him [*T.E.L.*] until he was brought to me at the Air Ministry and I was ordered to get him into the R.A.F. I disliked the whole business, with its secrecy and subterfuge.

H. M. TOMLINSON
1873-1958

5.xii.28   85, Waddon Rd, Croydon, England

Dear Lawrence,

It must have been in some previous life that three
men & a dog (the dog insultingly reversed) stood in a row with
Thomas Hardy in a Dorset garden, & you were one of them.
Must have been in another existence. I shall keep the fond
imagining, right or wrong, into the next life but one. (Far
enough to carry anything, says you). There was also, I fancy, an
episode with an infernal machine on the Chesil Bank: somebody
named Shaw called it a motor bike. I speak of these things with
caution, because you are such a magician at leg-pulling that one
is unaware that one's leg is off till you return that member with a
non-committal air, as though you had just picked it up off the
floor. (You ought to be compelled, for your sins, to read everything in the London press on Colonel Lawrence; when my old
solemn friends on the 'Daily News', for instance, get down to
your subject in perfect gravity, I love the dear old papers). But I
did meet you, didn't I? My wife assures me that I am not fooling
myself this time, to some extent.

For of course, though at times I astonish an admirer of yours
by admitting that I have met you (as though it were usual for me
to associate with signs & wonders) I know I didn't meet you.
The Seven Pillars told me that. In that book you made me doubt
whether you had ever met yourself, because if you had faced him
you would have had a hell of a time; there would have been a
shindy as though Michael & Lucifer had run into each other in
Trafalgar Square; we should have got out our air defences in a
panic. On the other hand, I have a suspicion that the whole of that
book is about exactly such encounters, & hardly a thing else —
a suspicion only, for I am by nature incapable of adventuring
into such dire contests, but can only observe the invisible combat
of the powers of good & evil with hope. Go it, Michael!
(Poor old Lucifer!). Something terrific, my simple soul tells

me, is going on in mid-air, & it is all for the best. Outside my scope!

I read that book with the closest attention & with pained interest. (In a true sense, all this excoriation of bodies & souls was my fault & on my account. No doubt of it. Me!). Your scenes I passed through with admiration & wonder; there was no doubt the sunlight was on them, though the light was both usual & ghastly. And I read the reviews of the 'Revolt in the Desert' (though I haven't read that version). Not a critic got near his formidable job, which might have been about a crucifixion, with himself as the sinner, for whom this was done. Romance, they called it. (I wonder what they would call a Christmas Story for Children by Mr Herod). Your Pillars could have been seen in no other days than ours. Significant symbols. It hurt a man to read that book, & it served him right; for he had to ask himself, My God, what are we going to do about it? And that, I think, marks another turning point in the long history of human follies. Nothing may come of it; but that does not concern you & me. Sometimes I wonder what would happen if full light fell on the scene & the words — so that all might get the revelation — 'Father, forgive them'. But whether anything is ever to come of that utterance, it must have been a biological fact & a necessity in the evolution of the species: not without import, if without relevance to our conception of cosmic affairs. I mean, if we cannot get it into our picture, the fault may be ours.

Which all I want to make clear is that you are less lonely than you think, & that there is no need, perhaps, for you to try to lose yourself in the swallow & maw of the military engine. I wish you were outside it, with the avowed intention to smash the damned thing. Why should you be broken twice on the wheel? Surely not because you were broken once? What have we done to deserve a witnessing of a repetition of the offering up of Lawrence? Dont overpunish yourself, for bless you, the punishment is communicable. The contrite monk who put peas in his boots (without boiling 'em) didn't know what pain could be; nor the virgins who used to eat muck & kneel on broken glass. If I could get peace & an assurance of being right by doing the last, why, I'd procure my horrid meal forthwith & smash a handy beer bottle for the curative religious rite. But if I could only get comfort by serving 7 (seven) years in the Air Force — Holy Mother! I'd sooner shovel coal in hades for evermore — much sooner. As to hades, I shall have no option. But as to the RAF, that — if I were young enough to offer myself — would be a choice; & I see it only as an institution deliberated for the destruction of the innocents — its wings are the dark pinions of Ahrimanes, coming by night to breathe into sleeping children the vapours of the pit. I hate what it stands for, as I hate whatever gets in the way of the light. Therefore, not the army for me, not even as broken glass for my soul's good.

And that brings me, not exactly to my reason for writing to you — I've felt moved to do that before — but to the immediate prompting. Edward Garnett — whose light the world will not see unless it removes the bushel — lent to me, with stipulations (unnecessary in any case) a sight of your life in the R.A.F. I declare that it is wrong in you to abuse your use of the pen when a spanner happens to be about. Damn the spanner. That is only another finger & thumb. I respect the user of it enormously — always have — but the engineer is not necessarily an object for respect: his work may civilize the wilderness, or it may, as I saw in a street near here one night, scatter a lot of kids out of their beds into the gutters. What is that? A bloody obscenity; & on the plane of the acts of some of the Turks you used to meet. It goes back beyond the cave-men into the minikin brainpan of the reptile. 'The roar of the aeroplane' (admired by some poet of the Mussolini school) is only a roar out of the Eocene. What is it to a man like you who hears the still small voice when his ear is so inclined? And how many are able to hear it, no matter how carefully they listen? There you are, with the ruthless mind of this younger generation, regarding the wreckage of a world ruined by the last of the Victorians — twenty-first century bugles to the reveille! — the altars gone the way of Pozières church, politics as obsolete as Joyhnson-Hicks (can't spell his name) & Birkenhead, economics as balled-up as the battle of Passchendaele, & the Sitwells & Frankaus posing for the Muses; and some scruple keeps you from sorting it out for us, as you could all right. There's this last document of yours. It ought to be published, naturally.

191

It captured me. There again is the eye again of this new era seeing things as our fathers never saw them. The young men would know what you were talking about — they would hear their thoughts aloud — & the old in mind & the obsolete would dance in impotent fury. It would help to make a difference. Come over & help us! You could do that whether you were in Dorset, Afghanistan, or Pekin. Do forgive this outburst. But nobody with a heart larger than that of a rat could read your MS without being riven.

Yours ever
H. M. Tomlinson

19.iii.30　Rigewood, Croham Manor Rd, South Croydon

Dear Shaw,

I got this pad with the idea of writing a long letter, for I was mighty glad to hear from you; but now it strikes me that it wants more of a pad than I've got, to discuss 'living' or 'life', & the mood of God on the seventh day. I'd sooner talk to you about it all. I'll say this, that if you've calm & poise, then its better not to disturb them. Happiness counts. Happiness is or ought to be, what life comes to. As for 'Yesterdays', my ghosts had to be laid. I was thinking of you, often enough, when I was writing it. There is a notebook here with reflections from the 'Pillars'. I pondered that book of yours. I was detached: yet considered, as an onlooker, while younger men bore the burden which was the heritage of their fathers, that I could not escape my share of the responsibility. There you were, once on a time, no doubt of it, involved in a mess you didn't make. The evil that others had done caught you, & you faced it for them — was crucified, if you like. That was what I wanted to show. When I used irony, my back was turned on you. I was facing others, including myself. Do you see? I was trying to tell them what they had done: a witness. Any good? Probably not. But one must testify, when one knows what a careless world did with one's friends, many of whom are dead. This thing <u>happened</u>: and there are those who cannot speak now. And it happened through evil & ignorance, which are by no means abstract. If you had not written the 'Pillars', I might not have been quite so sure about — well, say Oakley.[1] He was a good man. (His name was J. C. Faunthorpe). And he <u>is</u> gone. So there you are.

Do you ever come <u>up</u>, with time to spare? Wont you let us know, when you do? Our telephone is Fairfield 5760.

By the way. I have a son in New York. He is captured by Doughty's 'Mansoul'. He is, in his way, an artist: and is working at present for Harpers the publishers. He is <u>dotty</u> about Mansoul: he has drawn a picture of Mantown which <u>is</u> good, I think — and he has a notion of introducing Doughty the poet to America (his poetry has never been published there) with an edition of Mansoul which shall be a noble piece of bookcraft. His firm is reluctant, unless he can secure an introduction by one of the Great. My son suggests that the only possible introducer is — I mean you. Would I write to you? I would. But, says I, only two know what will happen if I do write — God & Shaw — so dont expect anything.

I should love to be in Plymouth, or thereabouts.

Yours
H M Tomlinson

[1] *A character in* All Our Yesterdays (1930), *a copy of which was inscribed* To T. E. Shaw. H. M. Tomlinson 10.1.30.

Printed heading

13.v.30   Rigewood, Croham Manor Road, South Croydon

Dear Shaw,

Go to! What's all this about being a born writer? Sergeant, this man has no birth-mark. Parading without a birth-mark!

Nothing gives me a more sickly feeling of fantods than to be described as a great prose writer. What does that mean? Didn't the Johnny get what I was driving at? What more does he want? It strikes me that the views of anyone unluckily known as a poet or a prose writer (stylist) pass as the odd idiosyncrasies of a fellow who has a rum knack with words: sort of playful way the fellow has.

Please remember your letter was written to one who read a book called the Seven Pillars. There were things in that which made me sit up; they moved the cortex. I'm not going to insult myself by recalling any of those passages, but I could do so.

And, you know, oneself is not a smokey glass, held (when introducing such as the 'Arabia Deserta') between Doughty & the public. I was one of the public. It was a worthy tribute, not at all smokey, that I read — was glad to read it. My stars, how many people were admitting the greatness of Doughty? I remember his death: it was one of the days when something big has stopped. And I would have gone to his funeral — I never met him — to stand at the back of the big crowd in acknowledgment of the sort of debt we owe to the men who justify human existence, now & then. But, thinks I, it would be silly for me to go. All the great people will be there. Robin Flower told me — he went, out of respect for a poet he had never met — that only a handful of people were there, in the rain.

This job of keeping the lamp alight allows of no hesitations about the merit of one's intervention. The simple truth is that your introduction to the 'Arabia Deserta' got that work placed where some of us wanted it to be, but hardly expected to see it. Cape was right. He knew what would happen if he ventured with the two volumes without your aid. It would have broken him. No doubt of that. (You say the book sold 4000 copies in England without a preface, but the copies which came in for review had your introduction — I cannot lay hand on my copy at the moment, for the workmen are in, doing reparations).

That doing of tangible things — I know the feeling. I like to stick roots in the garden. Polishing things — filing a key to make it turn — that's comforting & satisfactory. But a thought may turn to better purpose than a self-made key in a stubborn door —

194

open to honest men a prospect of the world they might not have found for themselves. Is that intangible?

Yours

H M Tomlinson

No Shaw, then no Mansoul for poor America; which could do with one.

SIR HUGH TRENCHARD
afterwards Marshal of the Royal Air Force Viscount Trenchard
1873-1960
(*Chief of Air Staff* 1918-29)

For his relations with T.E.L., and extracts from the other side of the correspondence, see Andrew Boyle, Trenchard (1962), *chapters XIII, XV, XVII, XVIII.*
About arranging a final meeting to decide the manner of T.E.L.'s enlistment, to which he had agreed six months earlier, but with the proviso, I'm afraid I couldn't do it without mentioning it to Winston and my own Secretary of State, i.e. *Lord Guest; T.E.L. then held a post under Winston Churchill, who was Secretary of State for the Colonies and Middle East. When he resigned from this post, T.E.L. wrote to Trenchard:* Winston very agreeable, hope your lord was the same

20.vii.22   Air Ministry, Kingsway, wc2

My dear Lawrence,

Yes, my Lord was very agreeable, but can you leave it for me to see you until after August 1st. Any time after August 6th up to August 12th will do to speak with you and it will take four or five days after that to fix up the whole business.[1]

The trouble of seeing you earlier is, as you will understand, with all this panic going on I am rushed off my feet, but if the

195

above address will find you I may get you earlier. Anyway, give me a date for talking with you and a date for the final plunge.

Yours ever
H. Trenchard

¹ *For the detailed arrangements made under his orders, see the letter from Air Vice-Marshal Swann.*

Trenchard wrote to A. W. Lawrence on May 20th, 1935: When he asked to join the Air Force in the lowest rank, though I tried to persuade him that he could achieve more in a more responsible position, he was so insistent that I eventually agreed. His influence in the Air Force was all for good in spite of the fact that wherever he went, impossible stories were circulated about him. *When the Press gave publicity to his enlistment, a crop of such stories arose and led to his dismissal from the R.A.F.*

29.i.23   Air Ministry, Kingsway, wc2

My dear Lawrence,

My Secretary of State tells me that you want to be given a reason for leaving the Air Force. As you know I always think it is foolish to give reasons!! but this case is perhaps different. I think the reason to give is that you had become known in the Air Force as Colonel Lawrence, instead of Air Mechanic Ross, and that both you and the officers were put in a very difficult position; and that therefore it was considered inexpedient for you to remain in the Service.

Yours ever
H. Trenchard

In reply to D.G. 189 *of the* 28*th, addressed to his secretary,*
T. B. Marson, but beginning: This is for the C.A.S., when he
is not momentarily burdened with big politics

30.i.23   Air Ministry, Kingsway, wc2

My dear Lawrence,
             Marson has shewn me your letter. I am never
burdened with big politics, it is always that the little politics are
the burden to me.
    I would like to agree with all you have written but the trivial
circumstances have been too much for me and for you. It is the
smallness of it that has brought about the decision to finish it,
and I know you will accept it however much you hate it.
    To my way of thinking, the only thing that would be of use
would be an Armoured Car Officer — Short Service.
    One of the drawbacks to you is that you have been a bit of a
friend of mine, and that has made it so hard for me to deal with.
    I will think over things, and if you could come and see me I
will talk over what I can suggest for you, provided my Secretary
of State agrees, and you want it and after investigation it becomes
feasible.

                                    Yours ever
                                    H. Trenchard

Written when T.E.L. was a private in the Tank Corps

6.xii.23   Adastral House, Kingsway, wc2

My dear T.E.,
             Your letter written on the 4th only arrived today —
the 6th.
    The Adjutant-General has arranged your leave most carefully.
At the same time, you must not be a defaulter or you will get

kicked out. Do not be an ass! If you start being a defaulter it will
be impossible for me to help you or for you to help yourself.

I wish I could see you again and have a talk with you. Do not
forget that I am always ready and anxious to help you. Best of
luck. Come in here some day & see me.

Yours
H. Trenchard

Come to the Air Ministry midday on Monday next — before
you return to Wool.

Upon receipt of a copy of Seven Pillars; *T.E.L. was then in the
R.A.F. again and due to be sent overseas*

22.xi.26   Air Ministry, Kingsway, wc2

Personal & Private

My dear Shaw,
I got your letters and also the book, and the part I
like almost best is the expression 'from a contented admirer and,
whenever possible, obedient servant'. This is a delightful touch
from the most disobedient mortal I have ever met.

Thank you very much for the book. I shall read it.

I am satisfied from my interview with you more than from
your letters, and I shall let you go abroad and not intervene.

I hope you keep fit but if you get seedy you may get sad and
if you do, do write and let me know, so that if necessary I can
bring you home.

You say you hope I shall not receive a letter from you until
March 1930. By then I shall have gone and others will be here,
but I will promise you that as far as possible I will see that you
can get out if you want to.

I would much liked to have seen you before you actually sailed,
but I suppose that is not possible, and perhaps it would be
inadvisable from your point of view, but if you want to be put up

for a night, my wife and children would be delighted to see you before you went out at Dancers Hill. Let me know.

Yours ever
H. Trenchard

7.vi.27   Air Ministry, Adastral House, Kingsway, wc2

My dear Lawrence,

How are you? I hear you are at Karachi, and I hope you are well and enjoying yourself.

Well, I will tell you some of the news from this end. Poor Longton was killed whilst flying yesterday. He was, I think, the most popular officer in the Air Force. Did you know him?

If Carr turns up at Karachi after flying from England, try and get a word with him. You will like him; he does not want to advertise or anything else and I think he is rather after your own heart.

Have read your book, and I must say that once I took it up, I didn't put it down again until I had finished it, or nearly did. It is splendid. I could see the blowing up of the bridges you describe! I have insured it and left it to my little son in my will. I hear the abbreviated edition has had a phenomenal sale and is doing extraordinarily well.

Iraq seems to go on its usual way — every now and then Feisal getting down in the dumps and then getting above himself. I suppose we all do this, but on the whole it has gone extraordinarily well and continues to do so.

No time for more, but let me know how you are, and if you are happy and contented, or if you would care to come back to the Air Force in England for a bit and enjoy yourself in the cooler climate. I could do it quite easily if you want to. It would be better for me if you did, I think!

Yours v sincerely
H. Trenchard

Answered by D.G. 354

10.iv.28   Air Ministry, Kingsway, wc2

Personal

My dear Shaw,

I have got your letter of 17th March, and I am sad.
I feel rather that what you have probably written is what is quite
comprehensible to you and to me as we both understand the
position, but it would be seized upon immediately by the Press
if they got hold of it, and they would say what a hopeless Air
Force it was — how badly it was run — what hopeless officers we
had, etc., when I know that is not what you mean at all, though
I have not seen what you have written. I am certain you will
believe that this is the sort of thing the Press will do if what you
have written is ever published.

And the Air Force is still young. It cannot go on continually
being abused by everybody, and I have enough of it as it is
regarding accidents and one thing and another.

I do not feel a bit annoyed with you. I feel I always thought
you would do it, though I hoped you would not. Anyhow, I am
going to see Garnett when I can, and I hope he will not publish
it or let it be published though when I have read it maybe I
shall like it?

You may feel hurt at this, but you should not be, as I am not
hurt at all about it. You know you did promise me years ago,
and it is not for myself I care twopence, but for the Air Force that
I have tried so hard to get going in the right way. I know there
are a number of faults in it, and so do you, but there are faults in
everything.

But enough of my sad feelings about this. I have many worries
at present — Iraq and the quarrel between Ibn Saud and Feisal
worries me a lot. I do not want to kill either side, and I am not
doing much in it, but people who live by raiding almost all their
lives do not understand our feelings on the subject, and they
dislike it when we try to stop them and think our methods are
more brutal than theirs. Equally, the poor unfortunate officers

and men who are in the desert trying to stop the raiding do not like it — it is unpleasant, and they always, I expect, feel that the faults are half on each side, like I do.

However, I hope for the best through patience and the Air, if I can only get the Ibn Saud fanatics to believe in it and to go up in it. If I can bring this about, I feel I may yet make peace between Ibn Saud and Feisal. Perhaps you will say this is impossible. Could you do it?

So many people get alarmed about these raids. There are rumours of 30,000 men moving, and rumours of all sorts of dangers — yells for reinforcements by political officers — some working one way and others another. It is hard to keep a firm hand on it all, and I am getting tired with having been 10 years in this office, and am beginning to wonder a little if I have done any good. Sometimes I feel I have done a lot, and at other times I wonder if I have done anything that will not collapse. Which is right?

My two little boys, Hugh and Tommy are nowhere near ready for Eton. One has chicken-pox, but is as merry as a lark and thoroughly enjoying himself, and so is the other. They are a bright couple and full of good cheer and cheek. Little Hugh says he is going to become an airman he gets very keen on it.

I am rather tired & weary & have been over 10 years now at this & yesterday the last joined told me how badly I had made the RAF & if he is right then I have failed but I am beginning to think that it was beyond my powers to do what I tried.

Best of luck

Yrs v sincerely

H. Trenchard

P.S. When do you want to come home?

P.S. In a letter to me you stated that all the profits of the book had been given to an Air Force charity & other people have told me this. But I dont know which charity & I thought there was only one & that certainly has not had anything. It is I know nothing to do with me but when I am asked I have to say I dont know.[1]

Yrs

HT

Answered by D.G. 354

¹ *The subscribers' edition of* Seven Pillars *had been produced at a heavy loss, by means of a banker's advance secured upon the royalties of an abridgement,* Revolt in the Desert, *the copyright of which belonged to Trustees. After paying off the debt, they assigned all future receipts to charity, by a deed executed on October 12th, 1928; in addition to their own signatures, it bears those of Trenchard himself, Lord Hugh Cecil and Lord Revelstoke. A total of some £20,000 was subsequently disbursed anonymously through intermediary trustees, the chief beneficiary being the Anonymous Education Fund of the R.A.F. Benevolent Fund.*

About The Mint, *the title of which he misread*

5.vii.28   Air Ministry

Private & personal

My dear Lawrence

I have never written in reply to your letter or your cable of the end of April or beginning of May. I have several times started to and always stopped. I have now read the 'Unit.'

I know I shall not hurt your feelings; it was what I expected to read. I feel I understand everything you put down at the time and your feelings, but I feel it would be unfair to let this loose on a world that likes to blind itself to the ordinary facts that go on day after day. Everything you have written — I can see it happening — the way you have written it is as if it was happening, but the majority of people will only say, 'How awful! how horrible! how terrible! how bad!' There are many things you have written which I do feel we know go on and we know should not go on, though what you have written does not hurt me one bit — far from it, and yet, if I saw it in print, if I saw it being published and being misunderstood by the public, I should hate it, and I should feel my particular work of trying to make this force would be irretrievably damaged and that through my own fault. I wonder if you understand what I have written. I think you do; try to. I read every word of it and I seemed to know what was coming each line, and I feel no soreness, no sadness, about your writing, and yet again I feel all of a tremble in case it gets out and into the hands of people who do not know life as it is. But as the Air Force gets more and more of the spirit I want it to get, so a lot of what you have written will automatically leave the Air Force without there seemingly being any alteration in the eyes of the public.

What I like in the book are the gaps. Where there are gaps, I feel you are content and happy.

I wish you could have seen the Display last Saturday. I very nearly cried over it; though the mechanics and pilots all looked upon it as their show, done by themselves, they were all so to speak patting themselves on the back for what they had done, and what they had done was the finest exhibition of what a useful keen, human being can do if he has the right spirit in him; but I don't think I could stand to see many more Displays. My little boy Hugh watched them and never took his eyes off the aeroplanes. He never made a remark at all, and every night he says in his prayers 'Pray God look after the airmen.' All he said when I saw him again that even was, what he liked seeing more than anything else in the year was the Display, and yet I am certain he viewed it with a puzzled mind — what was it it meant?

Last time I wrote to you I was sad. I am still a little sad and tired. I sometimes think people do not realise that I do not want to use the Air Force for killing only: the fact of an Air Force being about should in time ensure that we may not continually go on the warpath with as many casualties as we did in the past.

I have been trying in the past three or four years to work on how to improve the careers of the men and officers without it costing too much money. After four years, I talked to the Treasury for $2\frac{1}{2}$ hours and carried it through, and I hope to do it by creating a certain number of officers' posts and making more senior officers, thus making quicker promotion for them. At the same time, I want to abolish about 80 officers' posts in the junior ranks and add at least 80 warrant officers, so that really by this means I ought to improve the airmen's careers even more than the officers', as I am adding 80 to the highest billets they can attain to.

We are getting a very good type of man to join the Air Force now, even with the career we have had to offer them up to the present, and I feel that we shall hold that type when it is seen that I have added 80 to the number of Warrant Officer posts open to them. There is no reason whatever why a Warrant Officer should not do the work done by some of the Junior Officers, and do it a jolly sight better perhaps. Really, we ought not to pay officers to do the sort of work I have in mind — they get their money for doing quite a different kind of work. I wonder what will be thought of this? It can easily be criticised. It is hard to put the spirit into an Air Ministry Weekly Order. It is hard to make officers and men understand how we have worked at this during the last three or four years. I hope it will be my final work on their behalf. It is not perfect, and will be added to, and not, I hope, mutilated in the future. It will not bring about a splendid career tomorrow, but in another ten or fifteen years time the scheme will begin to make its effect felt, provided nobody pulls the whole structure down. It is sufficiently flexible to improve, but who will interpret it? I hope it will be understood and extended and improved as the years go on.

The other ranks personnel that are joining have been, I grant, relatively better than the officers, but I do say this — that both officers and other ranks are improving, and relatively speaking, we are getting what I want as far as I can see. If you talked to some of the young boys as I talk to them and see them personally as I try to see them, where they all have the respect necessary and none of the red tape I hope, I am beginning to think the type is improving enormously, and it is certainly as good, if not better than the army type. I sometimes go round — not as often as I would like — to see officers and men. I wish to goodness I could go as a private individual and talk to them more. I'd get a fund of information out of it, and I really think in a way they very often speak quite naturally, and tell me what they are really thinking and not what they think I want them to tell me. At least I hope so. I have now had eleven years — many years too long. There have been a certain number of letters recently — letters to the papers and sent to me anonymously, saying that I only care for drill. If they only knew how I hate drill and everything connected with rigidity! But it is awfully hard to get one's real intentions interpreted as one wishes. People will not understand that the regulation is only made for the fool to keep, but for the wise man to break.

When are you coming home? I have made up my mind to leave the Air Service at the end of next year. It is unfair to the Air Service to go on stopping, and I am not sure that I have not outstayed my usefulness.

I do not know whether you will get this letter at Karachi or whether they will send it on to you, which I hope they will if you are away, but let me know if you are fit and well, where you are, and whether you are coming home.

I am perfectly certain I am not really uneasy about 'The Unit', so don't think any more that I am. Your letter reassured me and I am certain you will understand my views, so I am pleased at having read it, and shall not probably remember it again in my life and time, though it will interest many people in many years to come.

Yrs v sincerely
H. Trenchard

23.viii.28   Dancers Hill House, Barnet, Herts.

My dear Lawrence,

I wrote a long letter to you a month or six weeks ago to Karachi in answer to your very long one about 'The Unit'.

Since then I have been asked at home what has happened to you because there were rumours about that you had gone to Afghanistan, but I said it was untrue. I hear you are with No. 20 Squadron at Peshawar. I expect you like that after Karachi for a change and I hope you have kept fit this hot weather up there. I know Peshawar well having been there for three years myself 30 years ago, and I loved my time there.

Drop me a line sometime to say you are in the land of the living. I sometimes feel I am very nearly being worked to death. I had one week's leave this year so far and I am going to try to get another 10 days. Do you ever get a flight over the frontier? Have you ever been up to Khyber? I was at Lundi Kotal for six months and enjoyed it immensely.

Yours ever,
H. Trenchard

30.xi.28   Air Ministry, Adastral House, Kingsway, wc2

My dear Lawrence,
         Your letter of the 11th to me from Miranshah Fort. Since then I have heard of you from Philip Sassoon.

I did not answer your letter on the subject of your re-engagement, because you said if I did not reply you would assume I agreed. I do agree to your extension for 5 years. I have also agreed that if you want to stop out there until 1930 or 1931 you may do so. At the same time, I am quite ready to bring you home of course, if you are at all seedy, and station you again at a place like Cranwell or somewhere similar.

I have cabled to Sir Geoffrey Salmond telling him I agree to your extension, and to tell you, so you will probably be told before you receive this. Let me know how you are and how things are going.

Now let me tell you this. Various people at home have been to see me, rather to implore me not to allow you to re-engage, but to bring you back to England. I have said that when you like to write to me or my successor and say you are tired of the Royal Air Force, I will agree to your going, but I will not take it from any of your friends that you really want to leave. This much I know you will do, (and you owe it to me) — you <u>will tell me</u> when you want to leave us.

Anyhow, the question of keeping open a permanent job for you for 5 years is, I fear, impossible, but when your time comes to clear out there is not the slightest doubt there will be lots of jobs you can get. I am not going to make plans for you 5 years ahead. But do you agree with what I have done — told them you are not available for any job as you have extended your service till 1935?

I should much like to see you and talk over things. My little boy is growing up fast. There is one thing you will hear by the time you get this letter, or very soon after, and that is that my resignation has been definitely accepted, and I leave at the end of December 1929. It is not, of course, decided who will succeed me, but I shall have done nearly 12 years by that time, and I think it is time for the good of the Air Force that I should clear out. You will probably agree, but may think it necessary to write and say you dont agree. Do not do this, because you must not get dishonest by stopping in the Air Force. It is supposed to be an honest Service, and I think it is.

Best of luck
Yrs v sincerely
H. Trenchard

16.xii.29   Dancers Hill House, Barnet, Herts.

My dear Lawrence,

As you know I am leaving on 31st December, and I am just writing to ask you if all goes well with you. I hope when you get my farewell message, which I am going to telegraph on January 1st, you will believe it is written privately, but it is impossible to put in cold print what I feel on leaving the Air Service.

Yours very sincerely,
H. Trenchard

23.xii.29 Dancers Hill House, Barnet, Herts.

My dear Shaw
        Thank you very much for your letter of the 18th.
Yes, come and see me when I am out of office. I am sad to go,
but I think it is the best thing I can do now for the Air Force.
                            Yours v sincerely
                              H. Trenchard

Written when Commissioner of Metropolitan Police

14.ii.34 New Scotland Yard, sw1

My dear Shaw,
        I enclose a letter that has come addressed to you here.
I don't know what it is about but send it on to you. It looks like
your own handwriting!
    How are you? You never come and see me and I hear little
of you.
    I hope you have read Groves' book.[1] I feel certain you would
agree with most of it. I have read all that Liddell Hart said about
you.
    Would you like my job?
    I suppose you are busy making speed boats? I hope you won't
come up the Thames opposite the Houses of Parliament in one.
    If you are in London one day, and I am not too busy with
Hunger Marchers (as I may be until they leave London) come
and see me, if you have nothing to do.
                              Yours sincerely,
                              Trenchard

[1] *Brig. Gen. P. R. C. Groves*, Behind the Smoke Screen (1934),
an assessment of air power and policy.

afterwards Field-Marshal Earl Wavell
1883-1950
(*In* 1928 *a Colonel;* 1933, *Major General*)

Sent with a copy of his book, The Palestine Campaigns
(1928)

Printed heading

8.i.28   Brigmerston Farm, Durrington, Salisbury

My dear Lawrence
          I dont imagine the enclosed book will have any
interest for you, but I send you a copy in case you care to look
through it.
          How do you like India, are you still at Karachi? Do you travel
India at 80 m.p.h. on that motor-bicycle of yours — Brough
wasn't it called? Karachi is rather hot and unattractive, isn't it.
          I like the Plain and this job very much, Im still G1 to the 3rd
Division. The Mechanised Force helps us a bit out of the rut of
ordinary peace soldiering. We ought to have an interesting time
with it this year, it's a formidable weapon of war.
          I see Allenby, Barty, Clayton and others occasionally. It was
sad about Hogarth.
          All best wishes to you for 1928. I cant tell you how much
pleasure your magnificent gift of the Seven Pillars affords me. It
is a constant joy to be able to read your beautiful prose. I am your
most grateful admirer
                                                  A. P. Wavell

Answered by D.G. 341

Printed heading

30.iv.28   Brigmerston Farm, Durrington, Salisbury

My dear Lawrence
        It was very nice to hear from you and very kind of you to like my book, at first glance. I hope it didn't disappoint you too much when you read it.

Im sorry you aren't liking India and are trammelled by bonds of self-imposed righteousness. I hope perhaps things are better now than when you wrote. I see they burnt a considerable portion of Karachi a little while back.

We had an E.E.F.[1] dinner last Tuesday, about 80 turned up and we had quite a cheery evening. Bertie Clayton is at Jeddah negotiating with Ibn Saud, and neither Barty nor Guy Dawnay turned up for some reason.

<u>Oxford May 1st</u>
We are doing a War Office exercise here, there are so many Great Ones that there seems to be hardly enough work to get down to Divisions, but we have spent a very pleasant day in the country, and shall I hope have another tomorrow. The Army is at last getting down to really good liaison with the R.A.F., a difficult problem but I think one in which we really are beginning to improve.

Cant you get sent home to Salisbury Plain?

                                                        Yrs
                                                A. P. Wavell

[1] *Egypt Expeditionary Force.*

15.viii.33   Blackdown House, Deepcut Camp,
                                        near Aldershot

My dear Lawrence
        I have a slack time for the next 10 days or so before
we go off to the Plain for training. If you are still at Hythe,
would there be any chance of seeing you if I motored over?
Would there be any chance of your giving me a ride in one of
your speed boats, which I should be very interested to see. Or
would you care to come over here and see us? It would be very
nice to see you again.
        Ive just been reading Young's book.[1] Your methods of war
rather shocked him, didn't they? He was at a private school with
me, and I never saw him again till we met once at a Disarmament
Conference at Geneva.
        Hope you are well

                                                Yrs
                                        A. P. Wavell

[1] *Sir Hubert W. Young*, The Independent Arab (1933),
partly describing his experiences in the Arab campaign.

H. G. WELLS
1866-1946

Upon receipt of a subscriber's copy of Seven Pillars

Printed heading

17.v.27   4, Whitehall Court, (Flat 120) sw1

My dear Shaw who was Lawrence

I accept the gift of the book gladly, the more so as after all I find it was paid for.[1] But you have given it me all the same. Do you know it has to be locked up & put away in a safe place at Easter. A kind of fury has come upon 'collectors' & sums like 400 guineas are being paid for copies. Damn collectors, who make a man hide in a safe, the glory of his library! They will steal. One cannot trust one's home.

I shall write to you a lot about that book later but at present there it is locked away & I am leading the most painful of lives in London. I am stricken & defeated. I really didnt think God could hurt me very badly — me being a cockney & elastic but he has found a way to do so. That little wife of mine who is a part of my past, a part of myself, who was clambering about on ski this winter, is suddenly found to be in an advanced state of cancer. She probably has less than a year to live[2] & some of that may be painful. It shan't be too painful for her anyhow. I just have to save all the time that is left to make her happy & content

I am writing a book of treason called The Open Conspiracy & I shall send that to you myself Such a lot of us want to make this present world feel the fool it is, & none of us really get together

Yours

H.G.

---

[1] *A notebook, in which T.E.L. entered particulars of the first* 98 *applicants, lists Wells as* Accepted 12-vii-24 [not paid, nor asked to pay], *but on the final summary of recipients his name appears*

among the Subscribers. (*These documents were bought at the London Library auction in* 1960 *for presentation to Harvard University.*)
    ² *Much less, in the event.*

W. B. YEATS
1865-1939

Upon his nomination of T.E.L. to the new Irish Academy of Letters — by virtue of being the son of an Irishman

Printed heading

Feb 26 [*Sept.* 26, 1932]   Riversdale, Willbrook,
                                                 Rathfarnham, Dublin

Dear Mr Shaw
        Your acceptance of our nomination¹ has given me great pleasure, for you are among my chief of men, being one of the few charming and gallant figures of our time, & as considerable in intellect as in gallantry & charm. I thank you
                                                                     Yours
                                                                     W B Yeats

Answered by D.G. 464 *of October* 12*th*, 1932: Dear Mr. Yeats, Your letter is dated Feb. 26th but this I am sure is Sept. I am a bad answerer but not that bad . . .

¹ *Mrs G. B. Shaw had conveyed the acceptance, and received the following letter, which she sent on to T.E.L. marked* This for information, *after underlining the third sentence.*

Sept 22   Riversdale, Willbrook, Rathfarnham, Dublin

My dear Mrs Shaw

Your letter has given me great pleasure. There was no man I so coveted as Aircraftsman Shaw. His name has been already accepted by the Committee. All the names I sent to Bernard Shaw have been accepted. The trouble about St John Ervine started because we had a name too many.

'The Irish Times' & 'The Irish Press' made the Academy the sole theme upon their posters on Monday. Today there is a letter in the 'Irish Press' from Lord Ffrench (or is it ffrench) who is some sort of a financier (we once thought of putting him in the Senate) describing us as 'the new paganism' & advocates of 'race suicide' & suggesting the foundation of a real Papistical academy. That kind of thing ensures the loyalty of our friends

I thank you very much

Yours

W B Yeats

INDEX

(The names of the letter-writers are indexed only if they are mentioned in letters not written by themselves.)

Stamfordham

H. M. Tomlinson

Harley Granville-Barker

Trenchard

Edward Elgar

Augustus John

David Garnett.

R. B. Cunninghame Graham